Gaining Archetypal Vision

Gaining Archetypal Vision

A Guidebook for Using Archetypes in
Personal Growth & Healing

Toni Gilbert, RN, MA, HN

4880 Lower Valley Road, Atglen, Pennsylvania 19310

Cover image by Robert Place
Text by Toni Gilbert
Images by author unless otherwise noted
Six Basic Guides for Dream Work © Jeremy Taylor
Kindness Has Strength © Serenethos. Image from www.bigstock.com.

Copyright © 2011 by Toni Gilbert
Library of Congress Control Number: 2011930194

All rights reserved. No part of this work may be reproduced or used in any form or by any means—graphic, electronic, or mechanical, including photocopying or information storage and retrieval systems—without written permission from the publisher.

The scanning, uploading and distribution of this book or any part thereof via the Internet or via any other means without the permission of the publisher is illegal and punishable by law. Please purchase only authorized editions and do not participate in or encourage the electronic piracy of copyrighted materials.

"Schiffer," "Schiffer Publishing Ltd. & Design," and the "Design of pen and inkwell" are registered trademarks of Schiffer Publishing Ltd.

Designed by "Sue"
Type set in UnivrstyRoman Bd BT/NewBskvll BT

ISBN: 978-0-7643-3911-0
Printed in the United States of America

Schiffer Books are available at special discounts for bulk purchases for sales promotions or premiums. Special editions, including personalized covers, corporate imprints, and excerpts can be created in large quantities for special needs. For more information contact the publisher:

Published by Schiffer Publishing Ltd.
4880 Lower Valley Road
Atglen, PA 19310
Phone: (610) 593-1777;
Fax: (610) 593-2002
E-mail: Info@schifferbooks.com

For the largest selection of fine reference books on this and related subjects, please visit our website at:
www.schifferbooks.com
We are always looking for people to write books on new and related subjects. If you have an idea for a book please contact us at the above address.

This book may be purchased from the publisher. Include $5.00 for shipping. Please try your bookstore first.
You may write for a free catalog.

In Europe, Schiffer books are distributed by
Bushwood Books
6 Marksbury Ave.
Kew Gardens
Surrey TW9 4JF England
Phone: 44 (0) 20 8392 8585; Fax: 44 (0) 20 8392 9876
E-mail: info@bushwoodbooks.co.uk
Website: www.bushwoodbooks.co.uk

Dedication

To my artistic grandmother,
Lilly Wilson Curtis
and
My mentor in the art of writing,
Mark Robert Waldman

Acknowledgments

My personal and professional life wouldn't have been the same without Lewis Judy, a loving and sensitive husband, father to my children and grandpa to every child.

Words cannot convey my gratitude for having been blessed with many gifted mentors. Some are also my closest friends who I turn to in order to think out loud. Like any good Gemini sun with a Uranus conjunction, I like to be around people who have expanded views of the mystery of our existence. They help me ponder my perspective on whatever role I am playing at the time. Friends who have contributed to this book in that fashion are: Billie Judy who has been around the longest; Robert Volkmann, my dream work partner and astrologer extraordinaire; Christine Payne Towler, an author and alternative practitioner with many years of experience in Tarot and astrology; my friend, Mark Robert Waldman, a wonderful mentor, and editor, when I can afford him. Elwood Newhouse always seems to show up when I need inspiration as does my longtime buddy Johnny Lake.

A few electronic friends were also helpful: Thank you Fania Chazen, a healer in Jerusalem who taught me something about Jewish perception; thanks also to Bonnie Cehovet, a writer in Washington State who is always willing to help out. And Marty Rossman, MD, a mentor whose pioneering work in guided imagery initially inspired my alternative path.

My newest friends are Lynn Keegan and Barbara Dossey, holistic nurses who understand that there are valid and effective healing arts that deserve to be acknowledged so we can get on with the business of researching and measuring their effects in healing.

Also a help in making the concepts in this book clearer are my reader friends: Sheryl Forest, Chris Giffin, Eric Dalkenburg, David Gasser, holistic nurses Deonne Wright, Susan Schafer, and Laurie Wilson.

Graphic artists Shannon McKibbin and Sara Judy gave us the visuals. Illustrator Robert Place came into my life to give us the beautiful cover art image.

The warmest part of my heart is reserved for Celeste Claire Sloane, a retired nursing supervisor, who has been a mentor and a counselor when I needed one.

After I felt done with my writing, I had a phone astrology session with Eleanor Kibrick in Arlington, Virginia, to check the transiting planets and what that might mean for this book. It seems that it is right on schedule.

Every form you see has its archetype
in the placeless world;
If the form perished, no matter, since
its original is everlasting.

~Rumi
Translated by: RA Nicholson in 1898

Contents

Cover Image Interpretation:
   Toni Gilbert and Robert Place 11
Foreword: Lynn Keegan, PhD 13
Introduction: The Unfolding of
   an Alternative Nursing Practice 17
Chapter 1: Archetypal Vision 29
Chapter 2: Archetypal Thought
   as Inheritance 38
Chapter 3: Archetypal Growth
   and Development 49
Chapter 4: Health as Expanding
   Consciousness 73
Chapter 5: Archetypes of the Community 81
Chapter 6: Archetypes and
   Patterns of the Archetypes 89
Chapter 7: Archetypal Tools for
   Healing in the 21st Century 103
Epilogue: References and
   Recommended Reading 121
Selected Bibliography 125

Cover Image Interpretation
Toni Gilbert and Robert Place

Temperance

The archetypal principles of moderation and integration, essential requirements for healing that bring our mental, physical and spiritual health into balance.

    Temperance does not ask us to deny our passions but to fulfill them in a way that brings balance, health, and beauty into our world. It is not about denying ourselves food or wine but about having these things in the correct proportions so that they bring pleasure and build a sound body. Instead of excess or poverty, Temperance teaches us proportion, balance, and acceptance the guiding principles in the arts. In the ancient world, Temperance was associated with the Greek goddess Aphrodite and was the virtue cultivated by artists and healers.
    Aphrodite represents the archetypal principle of love, desire, and beauty. Her Roman equivalent is the goddess Venus. At the lower levels of the archetype she is an unfaithful and deceitful seductress that causes chaos in relationships. However, at the higher levels she is a more spiritual love-energy that is involved in the healing arts.
    Dispassion is the feminine archetype of calmness that we center ourselves and call upon to quell the masculine fires of passionate desires. Thus allowing the Aphrodite in all of us to maintain a balance between vice and virtue, which provides a cure for our own imbalance and in this way we become our higher aspect.

12 Cover Image Interpretation

The archetypal Star of David being sacrificed to the fire is Aphrodite's commitment to a higher calling to become all that she is capable of becoming. With the green life of Nature at her back, and dressed in virginal white with golden folds, she utters the words "As above, so below. As you, dear Nature, are perfect, so will I aspire to be."

~Toni Gilbert and Robert Place

Foreword
Lynn Keegan, PhD

Gaining Archetypal Vision is a fine read. The introduction immediately pulls the reader smack into the formative years of the author. Autobiographical in nature, one gets a rare glimpse of a developing nurse and how the ordeals of trial and error, experience and practice, life's bumps of up and down serves to mold character one develops as they traverse from novice to expert. How fun for the reader to have glimpses into real-life situations, domestic life, and friendships in the search for one's own special practice area. It is these developed character traits then that foster the insight and practice of a professional nurse—a perfect lead into the content of an alternative nursing practice.

Sliding from personal experience, the reader gains insight into her alternative practice and then right into the heart of the book, archetypes—what they are and how they are experienced. We learn that expression in art work can give us important visual clues that hold deep meaning and value for the viewer. Looking at artistic images also causes feelings, thoughts, or other sensations to bubble up from our psychic depths. Tarot, one of the hallmarks of expressing archetypes, emerged from a collection of seventy-eight cards developed in the fifteenth century. The artful images on each card carry a rich symbolic tapestry of human experience. The author teaches us that art from these cards may be especially powerful if the image directly speaks to the viewer's personal levels of consciousness and development.

The reader learns about dreams and fantasies, shapes and forms, light and shadow, and then one asks: Does this energetic archetypal information exist throughout the cosmos? The old adage, "As above, so below" begins to take on a much broader meaning.

The history aficionado will appreciate the litany of facts from the early Greek period around 500 B.C. to twentieth century Carl Jung to even more recent philosophers. At this time in our history, we are re-discovering our lost intuitive arts. The author describes how the mind expresses itself at multiple levels from the scientific and material to the mystical and energetic. She also informs us that "when we tap into the *imaginal* world, we draw upon the energy of the archetypes in a seemingly collective or universal stream of unconscious information inside our brains, and perhaps beyond."

The case histories expressed in Chapter 3 brings the book to life. This chapter gives the reader an understanding of how to use archetypal patterns in healing. Using a case study we see how to apply nursing theory, i.e., Maslow's Hierarchy of Needs and Erick Erickson's Developmental Model, etc., along with alternative concepts such as the Chinese approach of Yin and Yang to archetypal counseling. Each example is pragmatic and follows with exercises for the reader to employ. In keeping with the alternative theme, extensive descriptions and applications of the Chakra system are described. Again, case study aptly illustrates the theory. Toni concludes this chapter by saying the beautiful words "that each of us has the potential to recognize the mysteries buried in our soul and as we learn to explore the *symbology* of our body's symptoms, the knowledge will help clarify areas of our life into which we need to bring more psychological and spiritual understanding."

Using the ever wise, perennial words: Health as Expanding Consciousness, Toni delves into Chapter 4. Again using case study, we see how the author blends imagery with chakra therapy, relaxation, and meditation to counsel a client through a maze of physical ailments back into balance. Many health professionals know that clients come to therapeutic resolution quicker when healing arts techniques and *symbology* are integrated with conventional care. We know that health is achieved through working through difficult life challenges like disease and death. Crisis gives people the opportunity to become more aware as they work through their life's lessons and grow to the next level of their development. This is known in nursing as expanding consciousness. Consciousness must be accounted for in all descriptions of reality. Beneath and beyond the brain's anatomical and chemical strata, there is a level on which consciousness is the primary force. What a delight to read of this and see examples of this illuminating concept in this book.

Chapters 5 and 6 are must reads as Toni shares her insights about archetypes in the community at large and how the entire world has the same archetypes operating in it. For example, in Chapter 5, we learn about the *Archetypal* types of fundamentalist, conservative, liberal, and spiritualist and are again able to relate to the theory through case analysis. We learn how it behooves the counselor to know the cultural context in which the client lives because it gives clues to the direction that you want to move their consciousness. Toni tells us that "an aware counselor has a good understanding of the family and cultural systems in which the clients are embedded. With this knowledge it is easier to facilitate client growth and development and help birth their consciousness into the next level of reality."

Chapter 7 gives tools for healing in the twenty-first century. Exercises and tools such as Dream Work, Guided Imagery, Tarot counseling, Humanistic Astrology, Movement and Dance, and Archetypal Energy Work are all defined and discussed.

By reading this book, not only will you get a peek into Toni's interesting and esoteric professional path, but you will have information to begin your own esoteric journey that first must be done within yourself. Each of her chapters ends beautifully with some of her own philosophy and pearls of self-knowledge filtered from a lifetime of personal and professional experience. By reading this book, not only you will get a peek into Toni's interesting and esoteric professional path but have information to begin your own esoteric journey that first must be done within.

~Lynn Keegan

Lynn Keegan, RN, PhD, AHN-BC, FAAN is one of the founders of the holistic health focus in nursing and a well-known leader the holistic nursing. She currently works as Director of Holistic Nursing Consultants in Port Angeles, Washington. She has authored or co-authored eighteen books and scores of professional journal publications and chapters in text books. Her books include the co-authored text book, *Holistic Nursing: A Handbook for Practice*, 5th ed (2009). Her most recent book is entitled: *End of Life: Nursing Solutions for Death with Dignity*, Springer Publishing.

Introduction
The Unfolding of an Alternative Nursing Practice

"I can't believe you want to be a nurse," Billie said eyeing me incredulously over a steaming cup of herbal tea.

I looked at her questioningly.

"Nursing is so tra-dition-al," she continued, frowning as she rolled the T-word out, as if doing something traditional was *not* the thing to do. It never occurred to me to question the idea of going to nursing school. Never mind that it was traditional, I could handle that. I thought it might be a way I could help people.

Billie was my husband's cousin and my best friend. We shared many things; we were the same age, had small children, ground our own flour for bread, canned fruits and vegetables for the winter months, recycled religiously, tried to be vegetarians, listened to the Moody Blues and Dylan for hours and discussed religion and philosophies into the night.

This day in 1980, we sat in the cool springtime sun at the edge of Billie's organic vegetable garden next to the rustic home she and her husband built high in the mountains of the Oregon coast. With our long, earth mother-style hair and homemade cotton dresses, we must have looked like two young goddesses discussing what day to bring in summer.

Surprised by Billie's response, I answered, "I want to help people live their lives more fully. I feel like I have learned a lot and now I want to teach what I know."

Billie replied, "I am not trying to be a nay-sayer, I am just wondering if a non-traditional thinker like you would fit into such a narrow box."

Several years before, Eric, my three-year-old son, was struck and killed by a car in front of our home. This life-changing accident riveted my consciousness and threw me into a deep despair that only communing with the angels would bring healing. After much prayer and meditation, my world-view shifted and I received several peak experiences that showed me higher states of consciousness; alternative views from which to understand and live my life. Now, I was ready to go out into the world. I felt wise at thirty. "I can't think of another profession that suits me better," I said emphatically.

The oldest of six children, I was now married with three youngsters of my own. It seemed as though I had always taken care of others. Not that I minded, it was my nature to be a caretaker and I loved to nurture. I remember playtimes as a ten-year old when I would gingerly pluck bugs out of the mud puddles in our driveway and place them on hospital beds fashioned from tissue paper. It felt good when one "healed" and flew away. No, Billie was wrong. I knew nursing was my calling.

Mainstream Nursing

My idealistic sensitivities got their first jolt in nursing school. It was easy enough to get in, but once there, it felt like I was in the middle of a rifle range with the possibility that I might be the target. The nursing program was highly regimented like a military boot camp and most instructors seemed like drill sergeants. Woe to the student who made a minor mistake. One medication error and you were called before the nursing director accompanied by your instructor-sergeant and threatened with expulsion. It was a difficult year for our nursing school, after the grueling written tests, obstacle courses called skills labs, and critically monitored clinical experiences, we lost half of our class.

"I don't understand; I thought this was a compassionate profession," the students repeated over and over. It was to be the first of many indications that traditional nursing wasn't the healing profession I thought it was. I heard through the grapevine that the instructors intended to be tough on us because life in the trenches of a hospital or clinic was difficult and stressful. They wanted to pass only the ones who could handle the stressful workplace environment.

Almost thirty years later, the institutions are claiming that we have a nursing shortage. This is odd because the nursing schools have never shut down and continue to graduate hundreds of nurses each year. But I am not going to belabor that point. It is common knowledge that the conditions of the workplace are not congruent

Introduction

with the ideology of many of our nation's nurse-healers. Healing is a gentle art and healers are highly sensitive.

I was not entirely naive. Before becoming a nursing student, I was a nurse's aid in a nursing home for elderly people who could no longer care for themselves. The nursing home gave me instruction on how to do things like take a pulse, count respirations, and get a blood pressure reading. I also served people food, bathed them, and emptied bedpans.

During this process, I got a first-class education by people who were at the end of their lives. I remember the residents well; they were my first teachers in the art of nursing. A few of the elderly residents of the nursing home seemed to have developed to their potential during their lifetime. They had lived a productive and satisfying life and it showed. These elders had traits of thoughtful kindness, inner peace, and helpful wisdom. Even if they could no longer speak their eyes still told of an inner satisfaction and their patient charts gave hints of their successes.

However, it seemed that some lived and died without developing a meaningful life. Take for example, Lois, a hard-faced woman in her 80s who insisted upon wearing heavy make-up that made her look like an old doll and harshly distinguished her from the other elderly patients. Lois had been confined to bed for twelve years with an extreme case of osteoporosis, a disorder of bone metabolism in which the mass of bone is decreased. This condition caused her bones to deform and break easily. She was an ornery old dragon, barking fiery orders to the staff if she didn't get her way soon enough. I was somewhat afraid of her and she quickly learned to manipulate me into doing her biding. In return, she seemed to love me and somehow I needed that.

Lois never married or had children and was without kin except for a sister who died several years before. The stories she told me of her earlier life seemed harsh and barren like her. So much so, that she seemed to be at the top of her game deftly controlling the space around her hospital bed day after day.

Several years after Lois' death, and after developing my abilities for inner sight, she appeared to me in a vision. During a walking meditation in my darkened house, I felt Lois's essence. I hadn't thought about her in twenty years. Then, in my mind's eye, I saw her as a nondescript energy image. The image seemed to have a location in the room, floating to the left, just above and in front of me. Surprised, I greeted her and she greeted me back. Bluntly, I said, "What do you want?"

She answered, "I heard you do healing and I came to ask you to bless me because I am going to be born into the body again. If I receive healing it will ease my karma and I will have a better life this time."

Well, this was interesting, I thought. Was this image real or just a figment of my highly creative imagination? As I understand quantum physics, we are all like dream images. We just think we are solid because our limited senses conceive our reality in that way. Knowing this, I wanted to respect the image as if it was a legitimate request from a soul who had crossed over (and besides, who was ever gonna know). I generously gave her a blessing rite. I made some spiral movements with my arms, with the intention of sending healing energies. Soon, a white cocoon had formed around her and I intuited that there was a gestation taking place within the energetic womb. I silently wished her well and the image vanished.

My experience in the nursing home kept me going in nursing school. Because I enjoyed the nursing home, I knew I would love this healing profession once through school. A tough and determined person, I take a lot before I'll give up. I am certain that getting through nursing school had something to do with my Celtic ancestry and the fact that my family included hardy emigrants and pioneers. They survived and so would I.

In school, we were taught holistic theory as if it were a part of the nursing scene. We were instructed to look at the whole person, the mind, the body, and the spiritual. That made sense except the spiritual was interpreted to mean: Find out what their religion is and document it.

After graduation, I was disappointed and traumatized by the workplace. I encountered similar boot camp treatment from my first nursing supervisor. She dogged my steps, scrutinized my work and documentation, gave me pink slips, and never said a kind word. She didn't want to help me; she wanted to catch me doing something wrong. I was afraid of her and afraid that I would make a big screw up and be fired. I quit after just six weeks. My young and fragile ego could not comprehend what was happening. I translated her uncompassionate treatment to mean that something was wrong with me.

Did you ever do something that didn't seem to make complete sense at the time, but somehow you just *knew* it was the right direction? That is how I felt about nursing. It was never my intention to step over the traditional boundaries in my chosen profession; like a good book, my story just unfolded chapter by chapter.

Introduction

My job hunting began again.

"What is your astrological sign?" Pat, the lead supervisor asked during my job interview at the Child and Adolescent Treatment Program at the Oregon State Hospital.

"Gemini," I responded.

"Gemini," he said gleefully. "We have a lot of those. Gemini and Pisces make up most of our staff," he informed me.

Here I was, at a round table with six mental health professionals discussing astrology.

"I am a Virgo," Sue piped up.

Brenda chimed in, "Yeah, Sue, you're the boss, and you're job is to organize the rest of us."

The whole group laughed and began bantering about their astrology. They had an easy fun-loving rapport and I took an immediate liking to these people. I *knew* I wanted to work with them.

Thus began a new phase in my education in a most unusual workplace, a locked facility for emotionally disturbed children. The environment was extraordinary because the staff interacted openly and honestly with each other. Like me, most of the twenty or so people were all in their mid-thirties and interested in psychology, which spilled over into other interests like music and interpreting the lyrics of Bob Dylan. What I liked most of all is that they were conscious that they wanted to make a difference in the world. I felt like I was home.

The client population was between 5 and 12 years old. All had seen horrendous abuses. Most had been sexually abused and some had signs of an early mental illness. The staff were surrogate parents in a safe milieu. I was the nurse that the children turned to for medication to calm their frightened psyche, band-aids for cuts, or a sling for a broken arm. I monitored their medical needs and rocked them to sleep. Archetypal orphans, their stories wrenched my soft heart. In my time on the children's unit, I learned to accept patient suffering as something I could do little about. Eventually, I came to see that I could not rescue them and that their life was their journey and their karma; a valuable lesson that continues to serve me.

Two staff members were Johnny and Levera, the first African-Americans I had known. Intelligent, intuitive, and gifted therapists, they modeled what they called African family way of being together with others. This included the healing power of touch, like a hand on the shoulder at the right time and being mindfully present in a tender caring, quiet manner. For the children and the staff, their natural way of being provided a safe therapeutic space to express injured feelings. In this way, they brought an ancient concept of fairness and acceptance in relationships to our group. Many years later, they are powerful leaders in our larger community. We still support each other in our individual paths and they continue to teach me about racial issues.

Looking back, of all the people who worked at the children's unit, I am especially grateful to have known George and Alden. The workplace was not harried and afforded us time to share our ideas and our lives. I spent hours peering into the broad minds of these two men. Both articulate and interested in discussing transpersonal concepts from the world of Jungian psychology; wonderful teachers, they led my inquiring mind through the world of synchronicity and archetypal patterns. To top it off, they told me stories of their many esoteric adventures—like walking on a bed of coals and not burning their feet.

In return, I brought my gifts to the group dynamic, like my fascination with art and its symbolism and an ability to interpret dreams.

Alas, it was not to last. After a couple of years of incredible rapport, we began to become attracted to each other. Since some of us were married and the attractions weren't necessarily reciprocated, the workplace harmony derailed into the plutonic throes of chaos that was not always platonic. The archetypal survival mechanisms of jealousy complete with archetypal competitive scenarios entered our unique little world-bubble.

Even though I was friends with these co-workers, after three years of intense emotional highs and lows of the unit, I felt it was time to leave. I transferred to the adult section of the state hospital for the mentally insane. The old cliché, out of the frying pan and into the fire, aptly begins to prepare you for my next experiential education.

For the next three years, I worked closely with psychiatrists admitting patients to two locked wards. I was an eager student and quickly became adept at recognizing the diagnosis of many psychologically extreme states and the available treatment options.

Unfortunately, unlike the camaraderie of the children's unit, in this area of the hospital I experienced a very dysfunctional work environment. Many among the staff, including the supervisors, had egos that were overly sensitive and would feel threatened over the damnedest things. They endlessly blamed each other for any problems that came up. It wasn't in their self-concept to accept their own negative thinking as an unconscious transfer that was a part of "their" world view. After a year of observing this behavior, it was my turn to be the target of their shadow projections. Finally, it became such a bad experience that I decided I did not want to be a nurse and I quit the state hospital.

It had not yet occurred to me that there was an alternative way to practice nursing. I only *knew* that I had had it with nursing, as I knew it, and was determined to do other things. I had another option.

Nursing was but one of my careers; the other one involved my husband, Lewis Judy, who was highly skilled at woodworking. Using my artistic side, I designed the furniture that he expertly crafted from Oregon woods. We were a part of an arts and crafts renaissance in our area. At the time that I quit nursing, we had been in business for seventeen years.

For the next three years, I used my artistic side to run an art gallery in a building that I designed and had built for that purpose. Lewis and I were successful at showcasing our handcrafted furniture as well as the arts and crafts of others. Because our work was showcased beautifully, surrounded by paintings, pottery, and a multitude of other items, we gained the attention of many patrons, including the governor and a senator of our state. From these years, I learned the art of media promotion and how to be comfortable promoting others as well as myself. This education was to come in handy.

During the gallery years, I went back to college. This time I followed my heart's interests in art and psychology. Although I worked part time at the local hospital to keep my professional license, I *knew* traditional nursing was not for me. I took stock of my talents and identified with art and its capacity to express the feelings of the client-artist. With the intent of getting my graduate degree in art therapy, I entered a new phase.

Alternative Nursing Practice

About the time I was to graduate with my bachelor's degree, I took a weekend class in guided imagery from a student of the Academy of Guided Imagery. Inspired by the class, the focus of my studies and my career changed.

As a longtime interpreter of dreams, I was astounded to see the instructor call upon the inner imagery of a wakeful dream state and use it to gain insights about physical ailments. I remember the class example like it was yesterday. The instructor helped a student achieve a light trance and asked her to call upon an inner healer. This inner healer turned out to be a lion and the lion told the student that he had come to help her with her asthmatic symptoms. I sat through the rest of the class transfixed and in a state of awe.

Sunday night at home, a husband with back pain met me at the door. Lewis was standing in the threshold like a human "C" because one side of his back muscles was in spasm. I told him what I had just learned about guided imagery. With nothing to lose, we thought it might ease his pain.

He carefully and painfully lay down and I talked him through a progressive relaxation. Then I told him to take his consciousness down to the site of his painful muscle, and to describe what he visualized. In his mind's eye, he saw a large rock. He thought that this rock needed to be pulverized to powder with a sledgehammer that happened to be nearby. This done, and the powder cleared away, I asked him what this area needed next in order to be healed. "It needs heat in the color of fire," he said. I guided him to breathe in, see and feel the fire-colored heat in the injured area of his back. On the out-breath he was to breathe out any tension or pain. At the end of this 20-minute session, he sat up pain free without a trace of the spasm. We stared at each other in amazement. I knew I had a powerful tool on my hands. Whatever this kind of therapy was, I *knew* this is what I wanted to practice.

Three months later, I was thrown head long into the next chapter of this career (whatever it was called, I still didn't know). My teenage daughter, Sara, was severely injured in a traffic accident. As Lewis and I waited for her to be delivered back to us from her second surgery, my husband and I held hands as I talked us through a spontaneous imagery exercise. We imagined florescent lights that carried healing energy to her from a loving source. Later, I learned that this was already an energy and imagery technique.

During the time that Sara was recuperating in the hospital, I saw an ad, about a workshop, by a research psychologist named Jeanne Achterberg. She was giving a lecture and experiential at a nearby college and it had to do with the use of art, inner imagery, and healing. I couldn't believe my luck.

During the workshop, and having just completed my first term in a graduate art therapy school, I saw the potential to combine art therapy with the use of guided imagery techniques to help clients achieve healing. At the end of the workshop, I spoke to Dr. Achterberg about my ideas. She thought what I had in mind was the right direction but warned me, "When you take your ideas into the workplace, take care to not threaten others." This advice was to echo through my mind time and time again over the next few years.

I was to learn that whenever one does anything new, others would naturally be threatened.

In the hospital, Sara and I used guided imagery in her recovery on a twice daily basis. Most of the time we used it as a comfort measure because it helped her relax so that she would get the most from her pain medication. However, we also used it to aid in her physical healing. For example, Sara's left leg was paralyzed from a bruised spinal cord. We didn't know if she would regain the use of her leg. It terrified me that this beautiful child might have to drag her leg behind her and use a crutch for the rest of her life. Her physician explained to us that we should watch for any sign of movement in her leg and foot because that would indicate a positive outcome. We did more than just wait and watch; I guided Sara to see, with her mind's eye, her leg moving, a little at first and then full movement. The inner images she saw came true and she was using both legs to walk within two months. Did the inner imagery really work? We don't know, but it certainly didn't hurt Sara to hear her mother's voice guiding her inner consciousness to see images of her leg moving and to *know* that it was healing.

With this experience fresh in my mind, I entered the art therapy program with the intention of working with art images in physical healing.

Mainstream art therapy was another disappointment. The primary focus of the program was to help psychiatrists diagnose and treat mental illness and disorders. Because this would have been a step backwards, I talked to the directors about the potential to combine art therapy with the use of guided imagery techniques to help a client with physical illnesses to achieve healing. At that time, the directors didn't know what guided imagery was and were dimly aware of using art therapy to facilitate the healing of physical ailments.

After the first year, and although I received 3.6 grade average, the directors were giving me a hard time. To make a long story short, I threatened them and the hospital staff with information they couldn't grasp and they decided that "I" was a problem. I made the decision to leave the situation. Again, like my experience in the adult section of the state hospital, I had to credit negative projections and limited thinking for pushing me to the next phase of my unfolding career.

Like a rider getting back on a horse after being thrown, I had a strong need to get back in school. After two days of feeling sorry for myself, I applied to the Institute of Transpersonal Psychology (ITP) a progressive graduate school in California. When I received their information I was surprised to see Jeanne Achterberg's name listed as faculty. I signed up for my first class with Jeanne's husband Frank Lawlis who was teaching a class called *Image Therapy Training*.

Still smarting from the art therapy school experience, and in an airplane headed to my first class at ITP, I looked out the window. Looking down, I could see the shadow of the plane moving across the cloud tops. A multicolored rainbow made a complete mandala around the plane's shadow. Like Noah of the Old Testament, I felt comforted and saw it as a sign that the worst was over. I *knew* I was headed in the right direction.

Finally out of the mainstream, I wallowed in the attentions of Diane and Irene, my transpersonal psychotherapist mentors. Even though their teaching styles were different from each other, they both had holistic values that were just the right combination of intelligence and intuition for me. They were the good mothers I needed to hold the space in the exploration of my deep psychology. Like a child who had finally made it home after being lost, I talked, drew, interpreted my dreams, visualized, and wrote about my thoughts and feelings. With their help, I made plans and goals for my own healing and my alternative counseling practice. My first year was spent learning wellness counseling and mind-body consciousness. The second year I explored philosophy, religion, Tarot cards, planned my professional course, and wrote volumes about my experiences. When I graduated two years later, I was nearly recovered from my mainstream traumas. But, I still didn't know what to call my chosen professional path.

Still wandering in the professional wilderness, I took a year-long certification class from my teachers Frank Lawlis and Jeanne Achterberg called *The Uses of Imagery in Medicine*. I don't need to tell you, it was a delightful learning experience. As medical shamans we drummed, explored our inner worlds and received concrete scientific data for what we were doing. Again, Jeanne and Frank had an easy-going holistic teaching style that went a long way in helping students learn.

Near the end of that year, Jeanne asked me what I was going to do with my education. I told her that I didn't know and that I was not even sure what to call myself. Jeanne encouraged me to stay in nursing and suggested that I find out about an organization that her friend Barbara Dossey was engaged in. She said the name of the organization was the American Holistic Nurses Association (AHNA).

I attended the AHNA conference that was held, in Washington state, that same year. I met several nurses whose career paths were close to my own. As pioneering nurses, each of us had our own unique path, but there were similar underlying patterns. All had become disenchanted with the workplace and sought other ways to be caretakers. Like me, they had received educations outside of nursing because, at that time, nursing curriculums did not offer classes in things like transpersonal psychology, mind-body consciousness and the use of spirituality in healing. Again, I *knew* I had come home. Two years later, because of my education in transpersonal studies, I wrote a challenge paper for AHNA and received my certification in holistic nursing.

One of the first things I did after joining the AHNA was to complete my guided imagery training through one of AHNA's endorsed programs. In their first year-long training course, Terry Miller-Reed, RN, MS and Susan Ezra, RN were certifying nurses in a technique that used guided imagery with physically ill people. They called their business "Beyond Ordinary Nursing." With this certification, I had come full circle back to nursing. Terry and Susan were teaching the same imagery techniques that I had learned in the imagery class back in college. This time, I would continue the education and take three more advanced courses.

The rest is a natural progression of events that put me solidly on the path towards my own career goals and back to nursing. It has been several years since I received my alternative education and began to build an *alternative nursing practice*. I write this book with future generations in mind. Like a good tribal elder, I want to teach what I have learned. The most important and profound experiences that I have had on my spiritual path are those involving the archetypes in everyday life and in healing. I feel there is much for us to glean from this way of seeing and experiencing, and that by gaining this type of vision, life is viewed as a magnificent spiritual adventure.

This book will help you deepen your healing skills. After completing some of the exercises offered, you will learn to trust your intuition in your personal and professional life. I believe intuitive healing must first be well grounded in established theory and practical advice. In this book, I integrate nursing theory, contemporary psychology, neuroscience, religion, and philosophy to teach you how to observe and use archetypal information.

For many years, I have used insight-producing modalities such as Tarot, astrology, dream interpretation, and other shamanic tools to enhance my life and my alternative nursing practice. With successful healing stories, I demonstrate how a healer integrates an *archetypal vision* with intuitive knowing and the creative process. You will be richly imbued with an appreciation for the potential that a working knowledge of the archetypes brings to physical and psychological healing.

In summary, Archetypal Vision will:

- Outline the basic principals of human development and self-actualization in healing, showing you how to integrate them into your personal lives and work.
- Expand your awareness of how disease and health manifest at symbolic and energetic levels so that you gain new perspectives in healing.
- Teach about numerous healing arts tools and techniques that will help you gain knowledge of the archetypes.
- Offer descriptions of several archetypes to help you master an ability to see archetypal traits and archetypal scenarios.

My intention is to discuss the use of archetypes in conjunction with modern medicine. Throughout this book, my aim is to use stories of healing arts to demonstrate intuitive knowing and the creative healing process. I will explain how a counselor can hold a space for healing while they help clients' access deeper levels of consciousness for healing insights and solutions.

The identifying information in the case studies has been changed to protect the identities of my clients. Yet, the rich archetypal scenarios of the stories remain a true testament to the powerful energy behind the magic of the healing arts.

Through my own experience, I *know* there is wise counsel to be gained from becoming conscious of the archetypal images, feelings, thoughts, and scenarios inherent in our inner realms and in their expression in our outer world. I see our grandchildren benefiting from our explorations into this symbolic way of life. I can imagine an entire population that deeply understands the divinity from which the archetypes spring. And I can imagine a world in which health care providers lovingly respect each and every archetypal expression, helping clients accept themselves in their healing.

Chapter 1
Archetypal Vision

*Blessed is the empowered mind,
for it sees vividly into the world.*

The center of the sixth chakra swirled much like a whirlpool of water. Looking into it, I thought that it must draw its life from an endless energetic stream. In my mind's eye, and seconds into a meditation exercise, a field of red filled my vision as though I were looking through a colored lens. I suspected that this color represented my still-thinking mind and, as I became calmer and my consciousness deepened into the meditation, the red slowly opened up and disappeared. The imagery field became brighter, and a swirling palette of rainbow colors radiated from the pinwheel core of the circulating disc. A multitude of small gleaming chards were embedded within the rainbow's multicolored light. The moment that I focused my attention upon them, I perceived a magnified view. Up close, the chards looked like flat, jewel-like pieces of crystal. I *knew* they were transmitting energy.

This imagery appeared during a focused meditation that I created as part of my final master's paper for the Institute of Transpersonal Psychology. I spent a month meditating upon each of the seven major chakras (defined in Chapter 3) and exploring other realms of consciousness. For me, the symbolic imagery represented archetypal information that was contained at the preconscious and unconscious levels of my mind. My task was to reflect upon choices I had made in life that led me to seek a degree in mind-body psychology, and what motivated me to use the traditional role of the nurse as a foundation for that work.

Insights gained from this transpersonal process of meditation and visualization helped me understand the larger purpose of my career. I saw myself as blazing a trail with a transpersonal view which added something new to the nursing profession. At the same time, it offered additional opportunities to integrate my spiritual life into my work. The difficult terrain of this path, as pioneering scenarios played out, acted as a catalyst that enabled me to raise my consciousness, develop wisdom, and eventually embrace my spiritual destiny. Like many health care providers of my generation, I feel it is my responsibility and mission to bring new perspectives to healing.

In the imagery experience described above, several major archetypes can be identified. As you read through the paragraphs, how many major archetypes can you identify? Here are a few examples: meditation, swirling, radiating, pioneering, and catalyst.

While it is fairly easy to understand the definition of an archetype, to see them in the world and to put that information to use is more difficult. But once you have a working definition, you know what to look for. Still, to see archetypal expressions clearly, you must immerse yourself in the study of them and witness them in your personality and life around you. This book will give you the foundational knowledge to see the archetypes represented in the first few paragraphs. When you finish this book, return to the opening paragraphs and test your newly acquired archetypal vision.

Why Do I Need an Archetypal Vision?

As we develop our archetypal vision, we move our consciousness beyond philosophy and definitions. With practice, we increasingly come to observe the archetypes operating in every one and in every thing. We slowly begin to actually see that all reality is Divine. This type of seeing defies the critical judging mind and allows you to see yourself and your world in a magical way; a way that mystically suggests the presence of a highly creative Spirit.

The concept of the archetypes is not new. According to the twentieth-century psychiatrist Carl Jung, archetypes present as characters, images, plot patterns, rituals, and settings that appear throughout time and in all cultures. As he studied the ancient philosophers, he seemed to have developed his own archetypal vision. He saw the archetype as the beginning or primary imprint, the original pattern or model of which all things of the same type are copies.

The early Greek philosopher Plotinus (204 to 270 A.D.) saw the Creator of the universe as pure being-ness, something that went beyond existing as a material body. Plotinus thought that the Creator contained all realities in their basic archetypal design, or pattern, just before their actualization in our minds. He conceived of the Creator as a radiating energy much like the sun emanating light. This concept roughly corresponds to the Jungian idea of the collective unconscious, a repository of the totality of human learning in which the essential archetypes reside.

In our time, neuroscientific research has identified areas in the brain that account for many of the principles underlying archetypal psychology—areas that generate intense visual, imaginative, holistic, and creative perceptions of inner and outer realities. According to neuroscience researchers Newberg and Waldman, in their book, *Why We Believe What We Believe*, the brain is designed to give us our various traits that cause us to perceive the world, and react to it, in uniquely personal ways.

Quantum physicists, like Niels Bohr and Karl Pribram, have hypothesized that consciousness is transcendent and unitive, and perhaps even the "primary reality" of the universe. However, quantum physics research leaves unanswered the question of how our individual, personal "I" emerges. Amit Goswami, author of the *Self-Aware Universe*, suggests that the individual self is part of what is called in Sanskrit *maya*, the world of illusion, and that our sense that we are a separate self is part of that illusion. This, again, is supported by the contemporary neuroscience of Newberg and Waldman, which identifies areas of the brain that create metaphoric maps of self and other. In other words, we neurologically generate illusions of "you," "me," and the "world."

In my holistic nursing practice, I work from the perspective that the archetypes are the absolute essence before manifestation into an image or action—a formless energy, full of information and ready to represent all the *possibilities* of certain types of perceptions, actions, and feelings as well as physical manifestations. The archetype can also be defined as the original imprint on our brains, an impression of human patterns that shapes our behavior, thoughts, and feelings. The archetype has many levels of expression which may be conceptually perceived on a continuum that ranges from destructive expressions to levels that are passionately spiritual. This point of view assumes a concept of the archetype as existing inside and outside the body, pervading our body as it does the entire cosmos.

In theory, the *archetypal energy* is activated in the individual consciousness, by events and other influences in the environment. Archetypal energy gives the individual a foundation for personal expression. The archetypes each have their own energy, their unique purpose, and their own direction. They also have many different levels of transmission and can be seen as existing on a continuum from lower to higher. At the lower levels, more primitive expressions exist, such as impulsiveness and extreme anger. At the upper levels, more sophisticated expressions await manifestation. For example, one major archetype is the "warrior," a person fighting for what he perceives to be true. At a lower level he could be a brute without a conscience who, mindlessly, wants to butcher and maim. At a more refined level, he might be patriotic and willing to give his life to serve his country. His actions match his righteous anger. "Terrorist" is another term given to the warrior archetype or essence of warring. There are many other names that different cultures have used to identify the warrior archetype: patriot, mercenary, the great avenger, etc. The final expression of the archetype and its level of expression is dependent upon the culture, the characteristics, and the maturity of the person expressing this energy (more about the levels of the archetypes in Chapter 3).

Of course, this definition raises all kinds of questions. If archetypal characteristics first begin as a formless essence (like electricity before it is harnessed), how is it then channeled through our brain into manifestation as our personal and our cultural qualities? And at what point does our brain put our personal spin on the incoming archetype? Is there a cosmic energetic field, or body that extends throughout the world—and maybe the entire universe—of which the archetypes are a part? If so, what are the characteristics of its components? How does this cosmic body, full of intelligent information intersect with those parts of our brain that make us who we are? Is archetypal energetic information, which some would call God, the force behind our very existence and a part of all creation in the universe? What roles do the archetypes play in our soul and spirituality?

If you consider these questions deeply, you must ask yourself: Are the archetypal energies a part of a quantum consciousness field that contemporary physicists are exploring?

No religion or scientific study truly explains how our world works. Thus, what we can ultimately know may lie in our ability to observe archetypal patterns in their unique expressions. As we become familiar with the archetypal effects upon our world and our lives, the more we come to know ourselves. The better we know ourselves, the more comfortable we will feel in the company of others. All in all, the knowledge that we gain from observing the archetypal system makes us more aware. And as we learn to make use of the archetypes, we'll enhance our personal and social life, at home as well as in the world at large.

Archetype

The archetypes are thought to be formless energy that is full of information—the essence that exists before manifestation into an image, action, or form. The archetypes are available and waiting to represent perceptions, behaviors, and feelings as well as material manifestations in the world.

A good rule of thumb is this:

Something is archetypal if its essence can be identified throughout all time, and in all cultures and places around the world.

Jung outlined five main archetypes:

- **The Self,** the regulating center of the psyche and facilitator of individuation
- **The Shadow,** negative qualities that the ego does not identify with but possesses nonetheless
- **The Anima,** the feminine image in a man's psyche; or:
- **The Animus,** the masculine image in a woman's psyche
- **The Persona,** how we present to the world, our behaviors act like a mask and protect the ego from negative projections.

Although the number of archetypes is limitless, there are a few particularly notable, recurring archetypal images:

Child	Mother
Father	Trickster or Fox
Devil or Lucifer	Warrior
Hero	Teacher
Student	Magician
Healer	Fool
Wise Old Man/Woman	Sage

Archetypal Expressions

There are many conditions that affect how the archetypes are expressed. In my own life, I often use incense and music to perform yoga. This sets the stage for optimal archetypal experiences during the session, such as flexibility of movement like a practiced yogi. When we use our senses to view images, listen to sounds, smell aromas, move our bodies, perform rituals, and so on, archetypal activity is stimulated. They can be conceptualized as constantly moving and changing, dependent upon environmental influences, personal development and personal history.

> ### The Archetypal Mystic
>
> As you sit down for a meal, imagine yourself as a holy person. You may set the stage with a robe, candles, music and silence. As this holy person, feel a reverence for the food at your table. In the present moment, seek a true and deep understanding of the nourishment the food provides. Clear your mind and be open to insights and the experience. You may want to do something like the following:
>
> Immerse yourself in the colors, textures, and smells of your meal. Slowly place a morsel of food in your mouth and spend thirty seconds mindfully observing the flavors and sensations. Or be open to having your own holy experience and let your involvement unfold naturally.

We find evidence of the primary archetypes in myths, art, dreams, fantasies, poetry, dance, music, and other forms of human endeavors. For instance, myths and fairy tales are filled with archetypal events and imagery, which is why they provoke strong interest in children. The story gives form to what can be called an *archetypal scenario*. For example, in *Little Red Riding Hood*, her mother tells her to stay on the path in the woods; otherwise the Big Bad Wolf would eat her. You can find this concept in every culture: "Do the right thing or else!" We all know that if we don't do the righteous thing, which is to stay on the "right" path, bad things can and do happen. Some might call this archetypal scenario a cosmic law; others may call it the law of Grace. Still others would see it as a karmic principle.

Archetypal Scenario

With a pencil, pen, or on your computer, write a story without thinking of what you will write. Begin the story with *Once upon a time*..... Then continue to write fast without thought of where you are going with the story. Write for ten minutes and then stop. What is the archetypal theme? How does the theme apply to your life?

Art too, symbolically expresses the archetypal energy of the artist.

For instance, I had a client draw her symptoms onto a paper that had a drawing of a body. She drew her right bicep with a red band, indicating an area of inflammation. As the discussion centered on body awareness and how emotions store in the body as symptoms, it became clear that this area symbolically represented her holding anger in check. As we explored this further, she told me that her mother never expressed anger and so, she didn't have a role model for expressing this important emotion. This gave us direction for the therapeutic work that needed to be done.

Expression in art work gives us important visual clues that hold deep meaning and value for the viewer. Looking at artistic images also causes feelings, thoughts or other sensations to bubble up from our psychic depths. Religious art, in particular, often contains powerful archetypal imagery intended to rivet the viewer's attention. For instance, some old cathedrals have large Biblical murals painted on walls. In the past, they were used as a form of spiritual teaching for illiterate peasants seeking religious guidance. The priest showed the picture to the peasants and told them the story behind the image. Art is especially powerful if the image directly speaks to the viewer's personal levels of consciousness and development.

There are many representations of art containing archetypal messages. For instance, you can find archetypal scenes on the walls of the Vatican as well as on the faces of Tarot cards.

Tarot, as we know it today, emerged from a collection of seventy-eight cards developed in the fifteenth century. The artful images on each card carry a rich symbolic tapestry of human experience. For example, the image of the Emperor on a Visconti-Sforza Tarot deck, dated at 1556, captures the masculine archetype. On this beautifully painted card, a bearded male figure sits on a throne as his right hand grasps a scepter—a symbol of dominion—and his left hand holds a cross on a globe, which represents the world and the four directions. His head is adorned with an ornate hat, decorated with a large black eagle, the symbol of the God Zeus and also of the Roman Empire. All of these symbols proclaim his authority, and we instantly know that the Emperor has the will to act, achieve, and dominate, just as the role of any king or chieftain throughout the world.

Dreams and fantasies also contain archetypal information. They tell us about our imaginary and symbolic selves. One of my clients was in an abusive entanglement with a co-worker, and in her nighttime dreaming scenario, she fell into a boat that was tied up at a dock. The boat was full of warm murky water, oozing with dead and rotting worms. Water universally represents life giving sustenance and we are affected by the quality of water that we have available to us. Without good clean water, we become anxious, sick, and may even die. In one interpretation, her dream expressed negative emotional states that one can find in humans throughout time and in all cultures. I helped the client understand the archetypal symbology of the dream in the context of her life situation. After the client thoroughly understood the symbology and agreed on the need for change, we worked out a beneficial plan of action.

The essential archetypes of each animal species show up in the animals' patterns of instincts and behaviors. Many of their archetypal traits are found in humans as well. Meditate for a moment upon the grumpiness of the bear just out of hibernation. The essential pattern of the bear's emotional trait demonstrates why we use animals in our symbology. You might say that your boss was as grumpy as a sleepy old bear. Another example would be the rabbit and its propensity to cut and run at the slightest provocation. Observing a timid person's behavior in a tense setting, we might describe him as being as scared as a rabbit. Using symbols of animals and their traits is a non-threatening way for the practitioner to teach about behavior patterns and how they relate to the human experience. We can use pictures of animals to help ground the client's behaviors and also to offer alternative behaviors that can also be found in the animal kingdom i.e., courage of the lion and the gentleness of the lamb.

We must consider archetypal shapes such as the cross, spiral, circle, square, triangle, grid, and the pyramid. If we look further, we'll see archetypal rock formations, chemistry formations, flower patterns, weather patterns that all look like they came from the same creative hand. To the trained eye, expressions of archetypal patterns can be seen everywhere, and when you develop an archetypal vision, you can identify the archetype as a kind of blueprint of life. Taking it a step further, if you look at everything holistically, these patterns seem to make up our entire existence.

One then has to ask: Does this energetic archetypal information exist throughout the cosmos? At a concrete level, we live with a certain geometry—the shape of things and the way that different parts fit together—that comprises the objects in our environment, such as a ball, a ring, or dried food on a dish. We see this same geometry at work in the beautiful designs that nature builds, such as an orange, the growth rings of a tree, and the random cracks in dried bed of a creek. These same shapes can be seen through a telescope: Saturn and its rins and the geologic patterns on the surface of Mars. What we see above matches with what we have in our surroundings. Thus, the more we discover, the more we see that everything is of the same mold, the same archetypal patterns. The old adage, "As above, so below" begins to take on a much broader meaning.

Chapter 2
Archetypal Thought as Inheritance

Honoring the Past Brings Gifts to the Here and Now

Knowledge of earlier ideas is relevant if we are to use archetypal symbology in healing and self-development. It is important to comparatively study the collective nature of the concepts and realities that we sometimes take for granted. Any thinking that does not have its roots in our traditions may be short-lived—a fad that entertains us, but not for long. Concepts that are built upon by the generations are living inheritances upon which we can build new foundations and theories about life. Indeed, ancient ways of perceiving the world provide much wisdom. For instance, one can easily see where our finest religious traditions, with their perennial wisdom, can be used as a guide to help us find our way through the quagmire of today's troubled world. By keeping an open mind and comparing what came before us, we most purely manifest the archetypal scenario of *honoring what came before us*. And as we pay our respects to our religious traditions, we also learn to honor contemporary wisdom systems such as depth psychology and modern philosophy.

Let us take a short look at how the ancient Greeks methodically observed the physical world and converted their ideas into intellectual concepts and philosophies.

First of all, in their time, it was fair to question the status quo of anything: religion, scientific knowledge, the source of their own feelings and thoughts. All things and every person and expression were equally respected as having come from a divine source.

40 Archetypal Thought as Inheritance

The golden period of Western philosophy began in 585 B.C. and ended in 529 A.D. Early Greek philosophers were the first recorded people to explore major archetypal concepts, and these thoughts would deeply influence contemporary psychology and help us form the consensus reality that we hold today. Jung theorized that cultural ideas get deposited in a place called the collective unconscious during the ongoing evolution of the human psyche and that we draw upon this information at will. Thus by studying history, we can look back over the generations and study their teachings layer by layer—like the growth rings of a tree—until we uncover the primitive stage of our collective human development. The Jungian analyst Edward F. Edinger felt that we could see the archetypal pattern of self-awareness emerge as we manifest our questions and meditate upon possible answers.

According to his book, *The Psyche in Antiquity: Early Greek Philosophy*, Edinger thought that the early philosophers were much like the philosophers of today, except that they had what Buddhists call beginner's mind—a kind of raw innocence that allows for freer thinking. Edinger states that there was no criticism coming from other points of view because everyone was just emerging from a time when humanity had been deeply enthralled with the mysteries of nature. He said that the early Greeks "stood at the dawn of rational human consciousness" and were beginning to reflect on the nature of human existence with a "bit of objectivity."

One has to question the accuracy of Edinger's idea that these philosophers were just beginning to think of things that no man or woman had thought before them. Did the early philosophers really just think all those concepts up at a time when humanity first evolved? Or did these concepts already exist in our cosmic psyche which is pregnant with energetic archetypal information and readily accessible to anyone who chooses the path of self-development?

One must also question the premise that no "archetypal" rationalizing went on before the Greeks, who had the wherewithal and materials to write their thoughts down. These men may well have simply been in the right place at the right time; the first philosophers to have the materials available to preserve their thoughts for future generations. We know, for example, that the Mesopotamian civilizations going back to 2600 B.C.E. had sophisticated laws and ethics to govern the moral behavior of the populace. Civilizations like English/Welsh Druids of Stonehenge, dating from 2180 B.C., and the South American Mayans (whose society began around 320 A.D.) made numerous contributions through architecture and art, but unlike the Greek philosophers, these peoples didn't have a formal written language to pass along the intellectual rationalizations of their day. Be that as it may, it is obvious that they analyzed, compared, visualized, and rationalized.

Edinger believed that these early thinkers reached a stage in human development and were beginning to logically and objectively reflect upon what it meant to be human, that they were standing on a threshold, crossing from the primitive and highly intuitive human state toward a more rationalized way of thinking. Could this developmental stage not be a stage of collective human evolution at all, but of individual philosophers maturing to the point of self-development that Abraham Maslow called self-actualization? If so, the individual would certainly—logically and objectively—reflect upon what it means to be human.

Whatever the advancement, one thing is clear: The Greek philosophers were visionaries, much like the early Hebrew prophets. And, like the Hebrew prophets, they were enthralled with the spiritual presence that certain archetypal concepts and images held. The prophets expressed their visions in their particular style of language, and the philosophers expressed their visions in the language of rationalism.

It can be argued that philosophy and religion, are primarily psychology, the study of the mind and soul. Both embrace the philosophical investigation of a psyche exploring itself in a particular time and place. Interestingly, contemplation upon the nature of life and reality underlies much of what we think of as depth psychology. One comes to this opinion by comparing a history of philosophical thought to current psychological, mystical, and scientific theories. One can see that the archetypal concepts that held the early philosophers' attention are a living system of interdependent ideas that undergo continued analysis as the inquiring and creative modern mind wrestles with them.

As a group, three philosophers from the city of Miletus Thales, (585 B.C.), Anaximander, a student of Thales (560 B.C), and Anaximenes a student of Anaximander (546 B.C.) give us the archetypal concepts of *physis* and *arche*.

The word *physis* is derived from the root of the Greek verb *pheo* meaning "to grow," and thus refers to three organic ideas. First, *physis* is used to follow something from its origin through its lineage. Second, it refers to natural growth and developmental patterns. Third, it can refer to the generative power of the material world and nature's urge toward growth. Notice that all three ideas have a *movement toward growth,* which is a form of archetypal essence that exists before it manifests into the world. Early philosophers mention God and *physis* as being one and the same *power* to create things—an innate organic urge toward growth.

Other early thinkers who considered the urge toward growth include Democritus, who said that men's lives are determined by the twin forces of nature and law. Nature refers to an original organic and divine source. Marcus Aurelius, a Roman Stoic, said, "O Nature [*physis*], from you comes everything, in you is everything, and to you goes everything." A dictum of Chrysippus, an early Stoic, was "Live by following nature." Could this be interpreted to mean that we should live by paying attention to, interpreting, and using natural cosmic principles such as synchronicity? Consider how we might use the Taoist creative principle of *going with the Flow,* or the Zen philosophy that strives to live within a harmonious state of spiritual grace.

The other archetypal concept of the Milesians is the term *arche*. In Latin, it means beginning, principle, and original substance. In alchemy, the term *arche* is translated as *prima material* or first matter. Derivatives include such words as archetype, archaic, archeology, monarchy, and patriarchy. These terms refer to what comes "first" as the patterns, the prototypes of existence.

Greek philosophy includes most of what we call the archetypal level of the collective unconscious. During their time, the philosophers described some of the major archetypal concepts concerning the nature of our abstract realities.

Early philosophy was based on the concept that all of reality is divine, and that humans are a part of that divine reality. The philosopher of the day had a *religious urge* to enter into communion with the *Divine All that Is*. No one argued about the basic assumption that all things originated from one source. On the contrary, they argued about the nature of the one source. That argument continues today as we discuss the nature of God/Goddess/the Divine/All that Is. What is it and how does it merge with our lives at multiple levels of consciousness and manifestation?

The golden era of Greek philosophy lasted for about 1,000 years. It ended when the Christian Roman Emperor Justinian forbade the teaching of philosophy. Rationalistic thinking was driven underground and the period of religious mysticism began to supersede the science and rationalizing of the philosophers.

Major Archetypal Concepts Expressed by Greek Philosophers

Philosopher	Archetypal Concept	Greek Term
Pythagoras	Numbering and the Divine image of dividing and replicating	*arithmos* tetractys
Heraclitus	Opposites Turning into the opposite	enantia *enantiodromina*
Parmenides	Truth Opinion	aletheia doxa
Anaxagoras	Mind	nous
Empedocles	Four roots or four elements Purification	rhizomata katharsis
Socrates	Art of obstetrics	maieusis
Plato	Eternal form or idea Recollection of what was forgotten at birth	eidos anamnesis
Aristotle	Potential at the beginning and realization at the end	entelecheia
Zeno	Divine word into matter, reason	logos
Plotinus	The One, the mind and the soul	hen, nous, and psyche

Contemporary Archetypal Thought

The modern concept of archetypes and the collective unconscious are among the better-known theories of Swiss psychologist Carl Jung. The origins of his theory may be found in his earliest publication, *On the Psychology and Pathology of So-called Occult Phenomena*, published in 1902. From there, his concepts gradually became less tentative until he established a stable core theory.

For Jung, the archetypes were psychic content that had not yet been submitted to conscious elaboration; each contained the *possibility* of a certain type of perception and action. He noted that the complex of archetypal expression had three components. The first aspect related to personal experience and was linked to primary drives and instincts. The second aspect had broader non-personal or transpersonal features, and a third and more psychic one relating to our imagination.

Jung emphasized that the archetypes represented an inherited possibility of *form* and *expression* but not inherited content. He postulated that the archetype would find expression in an individual's life through that person's particular experiences. Furthermore, he argued that there were as many archetypes as there are typical situations in life.

According to Jungian theory, the source of the archetypes is an unconscious pool of information that we draw from as we live our lives. He thought that all people share the information contained in this pool, which he called the *collective unconscious;* he saw it as formless information that has existed since the beginning of human history.

From another perspective, in their book, *Born to Believe,* neuroscientist Andrew Newberg and Mark Waldman demonstrate that shapes, forms, contours, tones, and textures are arbitrary constructions based upon the visual centers in the brain and the mechanics of the eye. Since other creatures, such as the fly, perceive "reality" in different ways, it can be argued that archetypal forms are unique to human beings. The authors demonstrate that much of what we see may not really be "out there" in the world. Thus, the reality we share is due to human concepts that begin forming at birth and, as we mature, we build a consensus reality that involves a complexity of neurons and sensory mechanisms in the brain as well as interactions with others. With this perspective, archetypal ways of being—such as father, mother, child, elder, and so on, are innate as well as learned. It is thought that archetypes are patterns that are universally perceived by all people and are only slightly influenced by each culture. In the same vein, mental patterns such as spiritual experiences, emotions, a sense of the spiritual realms, ghosts and God/Goddess/the Divine are also seen as archetypal.

Modern consciousness research, in conjunction with many branches of science, is producing profound interactions between all levels of reality and a creative intelligence. Scientific explorations have postulated the possibility that our universe is not three dimensional and linear, but rather that it is a four-dimensional continuum known as *time-space*. With this perspective of the universe, boundaries between objects and empty space disappear and the entire universe is seen as one continuous field of varying densities. In modern physics, matter and energy can be perceived as one interchangeable body. With this new world view, our consciousness can be seen as a part of All That Is and not limited to the activities contained inside our skulls.

This raises many questions. For example, how might neuroscience and quantum physics interface? It may be possible that the same archetypal energy operating through us is a part of the entire cosmos. If so, how does the archetypal energy get channeled (if this is the mechanism) through the brain to express universal human traits like anxiety, love, and fear?

You can see that to study the archetypes we must develop an open and thus empowered mind. In this fast-changing world, we must strive to be more flexible in our thinking, and to make changes without the rigidity of our past belief systems and thinking patterns. This open mind enables us to release old ways of thinking and acting so that we can embrace new ways much easier. In the process, we begin to develop a fair witnessing mind that helps us stay relatively clear of any rigid belief system. Luckily, we do not have to know everything or have absolute beliefs in order to be able to choose a perspective and use it in our lives.

Developing the Fair Witnessing Archetype

Buy yourself a nice journal and begin the practice of writing to your self. Journaling not only reduces stress and strengthens the immune system, but it provides a safe place to express your deepest emotions. It is a tool that eventually develops the objective, fair witnessing mind and the ability to observe one's experiences without judging. The fair witness is an essential component of any spiritual practice. In observing ourselves from an objective distance, we focus our attention, maintain a curiosity, and a calm temperament as we look at whatever is surfacing in our minds and heart in the moment. If we can observe our experience, we can integrate it.

Knowledge of earlier intellectual and mystical processes and their expressions can be seen to parallel with present ones. Thus we manifest the same archetypal impulses as our ancestors. One can begin to see where and why our modern concepts of enlightenment, individuation, and self-actualization may have originated. However, if this concept is archetypal and we follow our own nature allowing a natural unfolding toward personal growth and development of the personality, we must eventually come to the same conclusions as the thinkers of ancient Greece. Does this mean that what we think is accurate? Or does this mean that our thinking is archaic and inaccurate? No, it simply means that these older thinkers had the same configurations in their brains as we do; their neurological wiring allowed for the same types of observations and concepts to emerge from the All That Is.

Like the archetypes, the neurological functioning of our brains also has a history as old as humanity. It stands to reason that we would have the same discussions that philosophers throughout the ages had. In such discussions we would want to know ourselves at broader and deeper levels. In the process we also grow in our ability to grasp more meaning from our world and our universe. In this growing we build upon the body of information that has come before us.

Still, not one of us is complete enough to see the entirety of our existence. We cannot see everything that exists; in fact, everything that exists is not perceivable. So we must come to the conclusion that no single philosophy, and no single religion, can interpret our Creator's intentions perfectly.

Our current task is to discuss the individual psyche's experiences and compare its evolution and development to the larger process of the evolution and development of the collective psyche. Furthermore, we must begin to understand how traditions influence our thinking as we move through a broadening holistic paradigm in health care. Through continued education, we expand our consciousness to learn how the current archetypal patterns of disease and health manifest in our lives. Finally, we set about the task at hand to heal ourselves and our world, making use of everything we know.

At this time in our history, we are re-discovering our lost intuitive arts. We are learning how the mind expresses itself at multiple levels from the scientific and material to the mystical and energetic. We are also, learning that when we tap into the imaginal world, we draw upon the energy of the archetypes in a seemingly collective or universal stream of unconscious information inside our brains, and perhaps beyond. Further, the archetypes can be seen as a form of energy that one can tap into with insight-producing tools such as art and writing. The tools are many but all of them are, metaphorically speaking, designed to stir your mental pool. They stir up the mud at the bottom of your unconscious mind so that you can more closely examine the deeper layers of your psyche. As you work with the multi-dimensions of yourself, you become more conscious of the things that trouble you and you discover new insights. In the process you become empowered to make plans for beginning changes. Theoretically, we draw these archetypal energies into our own personal consciousness and place our own brand of expression on them. Our incoming archetypal energy forms into expressions, melding into forms of personal behavior, feelings, and thoughts, all according to our psychological development.

To me, life at its essence is archetypal. All creatures, plants, shapes, and even the weather have archetypal patterns. As I came to understand the archetypes, I was rewarded by being able to see them everywhere. They continue to delight and inspire me. I have come to see that all of life's experiences—the joyous, the good, the bad, and the ugly— have a place in the scheme of things. Life truly is a grand spiritual adventure.

Chapter 3
Archetypal Growth and Development

Magical, Mystical Physis
My Innate Call To Growth

Grace and Chaos

Like all of Nature, humans develop according to universal patterns. Theoretically, *physis*, a Greek name given to an archetypal force, is one cosmic power behind the material world. We know physis as the urge toward growth. As complex material and spiritual beings that urge takes place, not only at the material level, as we grow into adulthood, but also at the mental and spiritual levels. To say it another way, growth of the mind, body, and spirit is a natural unfolding of our potential.

There are many ways that our nature unfolds. Two cosmic forces that help us grow are the large archetypes of *Chaos* and *Grace*. The Grace archetype dominates when one commits to higher values in their living. The archetype of Grace gives us feelings of peace and harmony with our surroundings. If you are in a state of Grace, good things happen to you and you feel blessed. You notice that the flow of your life is easier and you may experience lucky events. Grace in our personality expresses itself with an easy style because we are comfortable with ourselves and we enjoy life. The *Grace-filled life* is healthy and satisfying.

When you are out of sync with your natural growth pattern, you start noticing symptoms of one sort or another in your body and/or your environment. One symptom that shows up when the urge to grow is not heeded is chaos. The archetype of chaos happens when one doesn't stay on the upper path or upper levels of the archetypal expression operating through you. The energy of chaos expresses itself as random events that are unpredictable and uncontrollable and people have difficulty navigating through this mixed-up energy. Chaos in a personality may express itself with behaviors that are out of line with a higher code of behavior; confusion and depression may accompany it. How many times have we witnessed primitive acts (i.e., cheating, stealing, and negative thinking and behaviors) and then watch a fall from Grace? When one gets out of synch with *Graceful living*, negative feelings and negative consequences or what may be termed *negative karma* usually follow. Many of us have seen the stumble-and-fall act so many times that we can predict the negative consequences that usually follow.

One example of being out of sync with a natural growth is my friend Elizabeth. Recently, she complained about a low self-esteem. She said, "I don't like myself; I am always comparing my self with others and I usually don't measure up in my own eyes." Surprised, I gave her an appraising glance; she seemed like she was doing well. Not only that, but she owned her own business, appeared confident, and was capable of getting her needs met in the material world. She had a good husband and had raised a family but, she was telling me that she felt a sense of "unworthiness."

Since, I am my education and experience at all times, my nursing assessment kicked in automatically. Because of my education in transpersonal studies, concepts of Maslow's hierarchy of needs pyramid as well as the chakra system came to mind. Later in our conversation, ideas from psychologist Erik Erikson's developmental model as well as my own experiences served as a foundation from which to see and explain to Elizabeth how and why we need to develop.

Let's take a moment to explore how these psycho spiritual concepts might be applied to healing our wounded psyches.

Elizabeth, was developmentally in middle adulthood but something was lacking. She was taking care of the needs of the first three material levels of the hierarchy model and the chakra model. This meant that her developmental tasks followed a common developmental progression from the lower chakras/pyramid up. She had hunger, safety, and belonging needs down to a science. Because she was expressing a low self-esteem, I surmised that her development was stuck and waiting for spiritual emergence, a fourth chakra issue.

The heart chakra channels and expresses love and corresponds to the fourth self-esteem level of Abraham Maslow's Needs pyramid (see graphic on page 56). Because of her negativity, I understood that she was operating in the lower levels of the archetypes of her personality. Intuitively, I felt she was working too much at the material levels and not tapping into the more grace-filled spiritual part of herself.

Elizabeth listened intently as I explained this to her, "When you choose to think in a certain way," I said, "it positively or negatively affects the outcome of what you are trying to accomplish. In other words, your intentions set the stage for your behaviors and then whatever you are thinking and feeling will be expressed through your personality. Positive intention usually nets favorable results, while negative intention usually sends us down a path to negative consequences." Because we are capable of operating at many levels of our personalities, I guide people to consciously choose the highest level they can manage. I told Elizabeth, "If you operate from a higher level of the archetypes, you will experience luck and harmony. In other words, when you choose the integrity of the high road, things work out better."

Like Elizabeth, clients experiencing chaos that manifests as emotional suffering and other problems, are predominately operating through the primitive personality, or the lower levels of their archetypes. It is the counselor's job to raise the client's level of consciousness about her issue, discuss it openly, and brainstorm possible solutions.

Over a cup of tea, Elizabeth and I discussed where she was in her development. She had her material needs well taken care of and was ready to take on the challenge of the next level of the pyramid. I call these pivotal points, *divine challenges* because, although they are difficult and scary, they are a part of Nature's call toward growth. I explained to Elizabeth that this part of her developmental journey had to do with self-esteem or self-love. This is not a selfish or vain love but a true knowing of your rightful place in the world—a solid knowing that because you exist, you are valuable. I told her, "When you love yourself, you naturally love others." I went on, "Self-love is not easy for some to achieve, but if you don't love yourself, you won't feel worthy to work on developing yourself." I paused and then said, "Loving yourself is the foundation and the gate to the higher self or your higher consciousness—to wisdom." I watched her expression to see if she was listening and then continued, "However, learning to love yourself requires inner work."

52 Archetypal Growth and Development

"What do you mean by inner work?" Elizabeth asked. We talked about self-development and how to use tools like meditation, guided imagery, dream study, and the imagery on Tarot cards to develop a better awareness of the whole self: body, mind, and spirit.

To sum it up, I said, "When you first choose to do inner work, it is an honest searching for ways you hurt yourself and hurt others. There is no exact road map for everyone, but one of the first things you must do is learn to accept your flaws. When you learn to accept your own imperfections, you become more accepting of others. Our fears also present challenges to overcome. The journey to wholeness is a courageous one and you shouldn't be too hard on yourself. Whenever you commit to this journey, you become a self-actualizing person and eventually learn to employ the graceful consciousness, inherent in the upper levels of your archetypes."

"That all sounds good," Elizabeth said, "but where do I find the time to spend on self-development?" She sat back in her chair and let her arms hang limp at her sides, "By the time I have worked enough to put food on the table and pay the bills, I am tired and don't want to do anything."

I responded, "That is a common complaint and misconception. Inner work needn't be hard discipline but, instead, a gentle tending to the needs of the mind, body, and the spirit." Pausing for a moment, I continued, "Find something that will introduce peace, tranquility, and rest to your hardworking self."

With a tired sigh, Elizabeth said wistfully, "Like staying home, looking out the window, watching the beauty of the changing seasons, and doing absolutely nothing."

I nodded and said, "Simple contemplative quiet time works very well."

Elizabeth perked up, "I could give myself a day of rest," she said triumphantly.

"That is a very old way to achieve peace," I said in agreement. For a time, we were quiet and thoughtfully looked out the window at her flower garden. I *knew* we were both contemplating the quiet pleasures of spending time alone and in the healing sereneness to be found by just being with Nature.

Elizabeth's development at the first three chakras gave her the traits necessary for a functioning ego. Because her ego-development was complete, she was fairly comfortable emotionally. She was at an adult level of development and so she could operate fairly well in the world. However, a part of her had remained undeveloped into her mature years and had settled into stagnation.

Because Elizabeth was operating at the lower levels at the moment, doesn't mean that she couldn't operate at higher levels. To be fair, who hasn't experienced Elizabeth's stuck place? I knew her well enough to know that she experienced traits of the upper levels, too. But at that time, her dominant way of being was negative. I knew she must consciously choose, moment to moment, to do her work at a higher intention before she could move her thinking, feeling, and behaviors to a higher octave.

As a transpersonal counselor, my self-actualizing ideal is that clients find their own way toward the grace-filled peacefulness found at the upper levels of our being. It is my job to provide tools or healing arts, to help them on the journey to find their "true" place in the world. Some eventually tap into their enlightened potential and full-spectrum of personal power. This power may include the intuitive and the psychic—a full spectrum multi-dimensional Self.

However, instead of rigidly judging according to one idealistic standard, there may be a multitude of reasons that most people don't reach enlightenment or their self-actualizing potential. At the back of my mind, I consider other perspectives like the transpersonal concept of reincarnation: We have lived multiple lifetimes and will continue to reincarnate after this life. According to this view, we enter each lifetime for specific reasons, such as paying karmic debts from past lives and taking on earthly challenges that further our souls' spiritual agendas.

Since no one knows exactly why we are here, my dominant perspective is one of suspended beliefs (no grasping mind) in favor of trusting a natural course. I regard all people as a divine manifestation and believe that we are here, each for our own special purpose. For instance, Elizabeth's karma, or destiny, is unknown to me and I must consider that her self-development may be secondary to her soul's purpose in this lifetime.

Growth and Development

In the hands of a transpersonal counselor, who is oriented towards humanistic and transpersonal approaches in therapy, the models outlined in this chapter can be a helpful guide to uncovering lifelong problems. It can also uncover hidden talents to facilitate the client's growth towards their full and rightful potential.

Maslow's Hierarchy of Needs

In his 1954 book, *Motivation and Personality*, transpersonal psychologist Abraham Maslow studied what he called exemplary people such as Albert Einstein, Jane Addams, Eleanor Roosevelt, and healthy college students rather than mentally ill or neurotic people. He claimed that the study of crippled, immature, and unhealthy specimens can yield only a cripple psychology and a crippled philosophy. He uncovered what humans needed in order to grow and develop. Then, he outlined those needs into a pyramidal shape, a five level model of humanity's physical, mental, emotional, social and spiritual needs.

At the bottom of the pyramid, the base is wider and the first three levels represent the material *needs* we must have in order to move to the next step of developing and grow into fully mature beings.

First Level

At the *first level* are the literal requirements for *survival*: air, water, food, sex, sleep, homeostasis, and excretion. This is what we need to be alive.

Second Level

After that, the *second level*, safety needs take precedence and dominate our behavior. *Safety* needs include: security of the body, resources, morality, the family health, and well-being.

Third Level

At the *third level* needs are social and involve feelings of *Belongingness*. This aspect of the hierarchy involves emotionally based relationships of friends, family, and intimacy. According to

Archetypal Growth and Development

Maslow, most people don't develop beyond this level. At this level, people can be reasonably happy and so they become complacent and don't heed the innate call towards growth.

The following upper two levels represent higher level needs as we develop our spiritual selves.

Fourth Level

At the *fourth level*, everyone needs to be respected and to have self-esteem and self-respect. It is the normal human desire to be accepted and valued by others and many seek fame or glory, which is external and depends on others. At this level one comes to the realization that one must first accept and love themselves.

Fifth Level

Finally, at the *fifth level* the need is for self-actualization. This pertains to realizing what your full potential is and then realizing that potential. The requirement to attain this final step takes a strong personal commitment. Maslow describes this as the *desire* to become everything that one is capable of becoming.

Although, there are no true lines marking the developmental stages or strict order of developmental events, essentially, people must satisfy basic needs like hunger and safety before they turn their attention to raising their consciousness to include beauty, truth, and the development of their higher potential and self-actualization.

Using the following chart, you can see that the needs of the pyramid roughly correlate to each of the chakras.

56 Archetypal Growth and Development

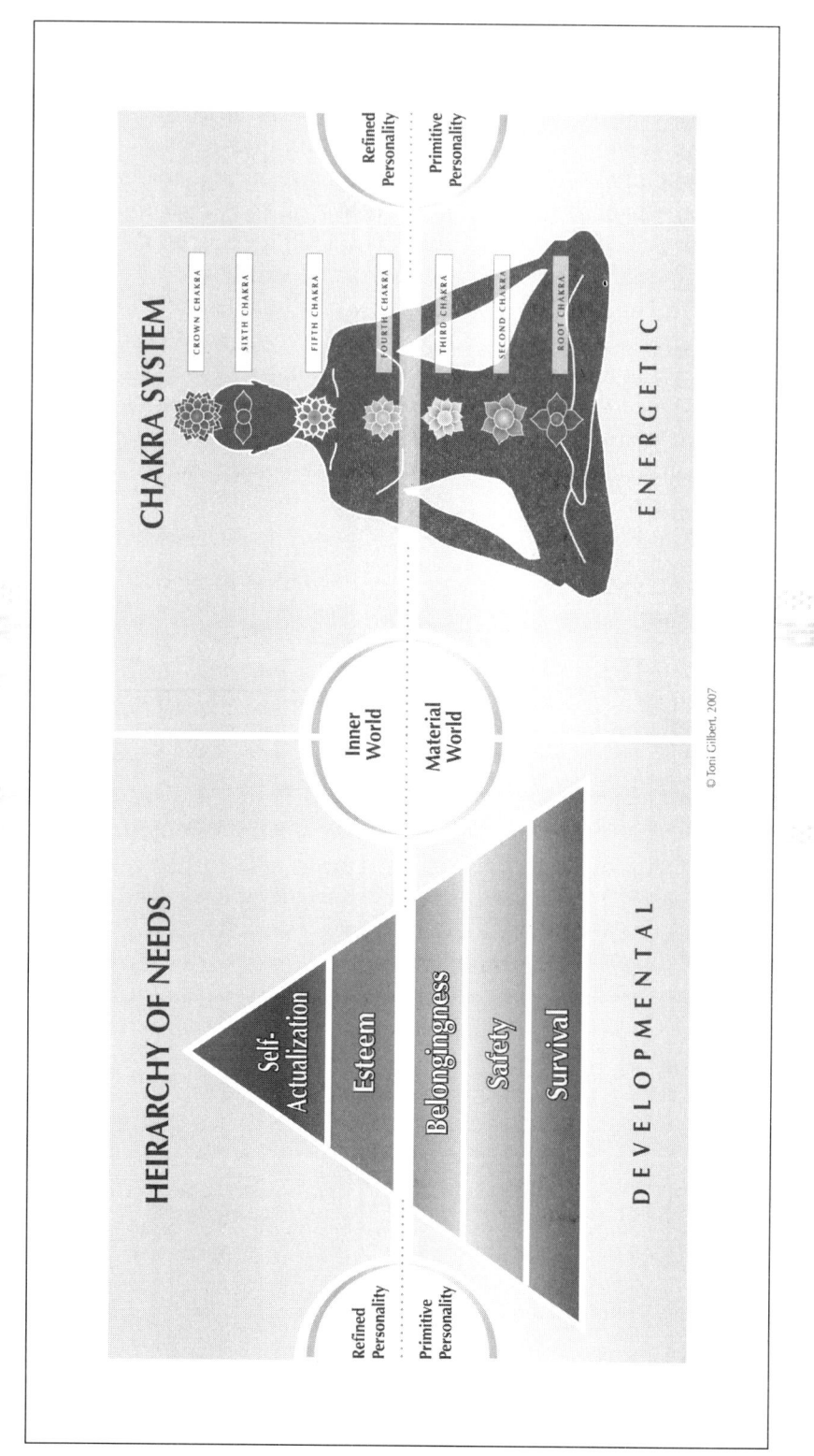

Self-Assessment Meditation

Place tape or paper on the floor to indicate levels of Maslow's pyramid. With soft eyes (closed but open slightly in order to keep your balance), stand at each level, focus upon that level in relation to your own life. Take a few minutes to allow images, thoughts, and feelings to come into your consciousness. When you feel done, step to the next level and repeat. When you are finished, record your experience. You may want to discuss what you learned with others or write in your journal.

Erick Erickson's Developmental Model

Erikson organized life into eight stages that extend from birth to death. The actual ages may vary considerably from one stage to another; nevertheless, the ages seem appropriate for the majority of people. During a first session, I watch clients closely to see how they express themselves in their dress, voice intonations as well as what they have to say. Sometimes, I may ask for a brief family history. This gives me a foundation from which to begin making the associations about where they are in their developmental tasks according to the eight life stages and correlations between the needs pyramid and the chakra system.

Erikson's theory assumes the position that the personality develops in stages. One of the main elements of his stage theory is the development of ego identity. *Ego identity* is the sense of self that we develop through our interactions with others. In other words, we come to know who we are by the way others treat us. If you are treated well, you grow up feeling good about yourself and think the world is a good place. On the other hand, if you were abused in anyway, you might grow up with low self-esteem and think the world is a place to be wary of others. Erickson also believed that a sense of competence is a motivator for behaviors and actions. If you have a certain competence, you feel a sense of mastery or *ego strength*. If any of the stages are not navigated well, the person will harbor feelings of inadequacy.

In each stage, Erickson believed people experience a conflict that serves as a vitally important point in their development. With this view, conflicts are centered on either developing a certain family pattern or failing to develop along the lines of those qualities. During times of conflict, the potential for personal growth or failure is high. If one fails to develop on the positive side of the conflict, it becomes a stuck place. At some point down the road, we must revisit our stuck places. We do this in order to heal conflict and develop a more positive outlook. It is only when one has successfully completed one stage that one can continue in a more positive growth pattern.

Erik Erikson's Stages of Psychosocial Development

Stage: Infancy (birth to 18 months)

Basic Conflict: Trust vs. Mistrust
Important Events: Feeding
Outcome: Children develop a sense of trust when caregivers are reliable and provide nurturing. A lack of this will lead to mistrust.

Early Childhood (2 to 3 years)

Basic Conflict: Autonomy vs. Shame and Doubt
Important Events: Toilet training
Outcome: Children need to develop a sense of personal control over physical skills and a sense of independence. Success leads to feelings of good self-esteem and autonomy; failure results in feelings of shame and doubt.

Stage: Preschool (3 to 5 years)

Basic Conflict: Initiative vs. Guilt
Important Events: Exploration
Outcome: Children need to begin asserting control and power over the environment. Success in this stage leads to a sense of purpose. Children who are allowed to overreach their boundaries experience disapproval, resulting in a sense of guilt.

Stage: School Age (6 to 11 years)

Basic Conflict: Industry vs. Inferiority
Important Events: School
Outcome: Children learn to cope with new social and academic demands. Success leads to a sense of competence, while failure results in feelings of inferiority.

Stage: Adolescence (12 to 18 years)

Basic Conflict: Identity vs. Role Confusion
Important Events: Social Relationships
Outcome: Teens learn to develop a sense of self and personal identity. Success leads to an ability to stay true to oneself, while failure leads to role confusion and a weak sense of self.

Stage: Young Adulthood (19 to 40 years)

Basic Conflict: Intimacy vs. Isolation
Important Events: Relationships
Outcome: Young adults need to form intimate, loving relationships with other people. Success leads to strong relationships, while failure results in isolation and loneliness.

Stage: Middle Adulthood (40 to 65)

Basic Conflict: Generativity vs. Stagnation
Important Events: Work and Parenthood
Outcome: Adults need to create or nurture things that they can pass to the next generation, often by having children or creating a positive change that benefits other people. Success leads to feelings of usefulness and accomplishment, while failure results in shallow involvement in the world.

Stage: Maturity (65 years to death)

Basic Conflict: Ego Integrity vs. Despair
Important Events: Reflection on Life
Outcome: Older adults need to look back on life and feel a sense of fulfillment. Success at this stage leads to feelings of wisdom and integrity, while failure results in regret, and despair.

Using the graphics in this chapter, you will begin to see how the developmental needs of the pyramid broadly correlates to the energetic traits of the chakras an energetic system of *consciousness* within and surrounding our physical bodies. I find it helpful to use both of these models in combination with Erick Erikson's eight life stages model. The concepts from all three theories complement each other and provide a framework for a pattern of growth—a road map of the archetypes and how they find expression through the person. Additionally, my broad education in human studies, religion, philosophy, and psychology, as well as life experiences also serves in client assessments.

Levels of the Archetypes

Studies of the archetypes operating through us are made easier by reducing them into two broad levels of expression so that we can better understand what clients are expressing and work more comprehensively with their archetypes. I have separated multiple aspects of the archetypes—or who we are energetically—into two categories: the *upper refined personality* and the *lower primitive personality*. Because we have different archetypal levels of consciousness, the energies of the archetypes are available to us to use in a dynamic and complex way. They are the behaviors that we choose to express moment to moment. We choose these levels according to our development, mood, thoughts, values, and environmental circumstances.

The Refined Personality

When people operate in the upper levels of their archetypes, they display more refined behaviors. When we access this part of our psyche we operate at higher levels of consciousness, which is sometimes called the higher mind. Here, we become aware that we can control and express ourselves in any way we choose, and because we are choosing to authentically display who we are, we may seem eccentric to others.

The upper level personality predominantly chooses a path of "right action," a Buddhist term that refers to one's ability to compassionately interact with the world. Such people are mentally and emotionally stable and have a high self-esteem. They love themselves and they love others, often demonstrating unique talents and gifts. Usually, they are idealists who demonstrate high social values (which may not conform to society's values) and actively or passively resist an unjust authority.

The more refined personality actualizes innate gifts and talents and strives to become all that he or she is capable of becoming. There is a desire to go beyond everyday experiences to explore the mysterious, the chaotic, and the unexplained. Those who are living predominantly in the upper levels are highly intuitive and spiritually in tune with something greater than themselves. They have mystical inclinations and enjoy physical, mental, and spiritual health. They are usually involved in worthy causes like the environment and spiritual teaching. Many times they are in the process of helping their culture evolve.

The Primitive Personality

If the lower levels of the archetypes dominate us, we express a more primal personality. Survival, tribal belonging, and social cooperation are the primary things a person strives for. When we are operating at this level, we are focused upon coping with life by gratifying our physiological needs: eating, sleeping, working, meeting basic relationship needs and maintaining secure shelter for self and family.

We seek affection from relationships such as family and friends, and although we may be cooperative, we may also be competitive and conditional in our generosity. We can give love but expect something in return.

When this level is dominant, we often aren't aware that we have an inner consciousness; thus we exhibit a more concrete and materialistic way of being in the world. We will also tend to display black and white thinking, dreading the unfamiliar and clinging to the familiar by seeking safety in an undisputed life routine. At this level, the world is seen as cause and effect. It feels like an unsafe place because we have little control over it; thus we seek to organize ourselves around rules and ceremonies. This pragmatic mind-set has a belief system or a religion that gives organized answers to an organized universe.

At these lower levels, our traits include aggression, fear, cruelty, manipulation, lying, dependence, victimization, fanaticism towards a religious doctrine or a cause, and a lack of empathy towards others. We may find ourselves ill, addicted, or beset by social and psychological problems.

The Chakra System

The chakra system is a traditional energy model that has been used throughout Asia for centuries. The chakras are energy centers that form the coordinating network of our complicated mind-body system. All our actions and understandings are thought to arise from these multiple points of energy within ourselves. Full of archetypal information, they are thought to form connecting links between mind, body, spirit, past and future as well as the energy of the cosmos. The chakra system provides an excellent framework for assessing not only the mind and body but also the spiritual aspects of a person.

The following is a summary of the larger chakras and the psychological, physical, and spiritual effects. Knowledge and skilled use of this model goes a long way in helping people recover from illness and injury. It is a map of body consciousness that, with patience and clear intent, our imaginations move the magic of healing energy through our bodies to heal our infirmities and to keep us healthy.

Lower Material Level Chakras

First Chakra

The *first chakra* is the seat of desire and consciousness of the physical body. This root chakra is located somewhere between the base of the spine and the genitals. It is the energy grounding us to our bodies and the world around us. With a disrupted flow of energy, we feel weak and ungrounded. If this energy is strong it provides us with a strong emotional foundation, which is needed for everything that is of this world.

Provides energy to: nervous system, immune system, bones, base of spine, buttocks, genitals, pelvic area, bladder and intestines, legs and feet.

Archetypal principles: primal fear, anxiety, feeling at home, sex, eating, bodily functions, survival. This chakra energy manifests in the imagination as feelings of safety and movement.

Upper levels: ability to manage fear and anxiety, comfortable in the world, enjoy the pleasures of the body, have no difficulties with bodily functions, able to provide safety for yourself, feelings of safety and satiety, touch says love to you.

Lower levels: fear driven, anxious, mental illness, dysfunctional sex life, addictions, incapacitated, touch hunger, psychosis.

Second Chakra

The *second chakra* is the seat of sensuality and feelings and is located about two inches below the navel. Through our connection to others we experience, passion, movement, transformation, and intimacy. If the energy is healthy, it flows unimpeded and we experience sensible relationships.

Provides energy to: the reproductive organs, large intestines, adrenal glands, lower vertebrae, pelvis and hips, appendix, kidneys, and the bladder.

Archetypal principles: social situations, belonging, ethics, creativity, power and control, blame and guilt, physiological gratification. Inner images include activities such as fighting or socializing.

Upper levels: enjoys the company of others and has friends, stands by a cause, good work ethic, good planning skills, sublimate control issues by manipulating the environment rather than others, sexually competent, creativity, chosen celibacy.

Lower levels: an infantile possessive love, social dysfunctions, loner, needs rules and regulations, lacks creativity, need to control others, blames others, lack of remorse, impotence.

Third Chakra

The *third chakra* is the seat of the ego or sense of self and worldly values and is located a few inches above the naval. When we have what you might call strong or weak personality traits or a low self-esteem, we are weak in this chakra energy. The chakra is strong when we respond with pride to an accomplishment and we feel a strong personal power.

Provides energy to: the abdomen, stomach, upper intestines, liver, spleen, gallbladder, kidney, pancreas, and the middle spine

Archetypal principles: basic socialization, logical personality types, simple logic, concrete thinking. The archetypal images, of the imagination, have more of a personality and may appear in your imagination as someone you know. They bring information to help us operate in the world in some archetypal function.

Upper levels: follows the rules, honest business dealings, makes fair rules, controls his animal nature, choices based on logic, trustworthy, good social graces, help others but expect something in return, open minded.

Lower levels: black and white good versus bad thinking, dishonest, may cheat in business, influenced by friends, unequal treatment of fellow workers, lies without cause, is late, sexually promiscuous, thoughtless of others, one dimension of ego awareness.

Upper Spiritual Level Chakras

Fourth Chakra

The *fourth chakra* is the seat of the heart and is located in the middle of the chest. The energy here becomes less dense and is more feeling in nature. There is a consciousness merging between the energetic body and the material one. Weak energy here would manifest as emotional dysfunction. Strong energy is present when there is harmony within and is expressed as love and compassion.

Provides energy to: the heart, esophagus, stomach, liver, lungs, upper back, arms, shoulders and hands.

Archetypal principles: altruism, yin and yang of balanced energy, poetry, healing, artistic creativity, nursing others compassionately, compassion, love, kindness, joy, harmony, emotional warmth, androgyny, mystical experiences.

Upper levels: values the spiritual, affairs of the heart, self-sacrifice for the right reasons. Images demonstrate positive feminine principles such as Isis, Diana, and Mary Magdalene, the masculine principal seeking spiritual reform such as Jesus and Buddha, religious pilgrimages.

Lower levels: resentfully nursing others, suffering, illicit love affairs, flirtation, lack of self-love, inability to love others, self-sacrifice for the wrong reasons, emotional problems. Archetypal images are sexy love types. For example, women like Jane Mansfield and Marilyn Monroe and superficial playboy types like Don Juan and Peter Pan.

Fifth Chakra

The *fifth chakra* is the seat of the will and may be found in the upper chest, neck, and throat area. Weakness in this area results in addictions and inability to express oneself. Ultimately the strength gained in this area is used to do the will of the cosmos and you begin to communicate with the passion of an angel.

Provides energy to: the mouth, teeth, lips, thyroid, tongue, throat, ears and lower sinuses, upper spine, neck.

Archetypal principles: creative urges, determination to finish what you set out to do, motivational speaking, writing, singing and transpersonal counseling. People who have made use of this chakra are Joan Baez, Bob Dylan, and the poet Kahlil Gibran. Inner imagery is manifest as beings (including you) who are adept at this level of operation. The imagery may also include members of the animal kingdom.

Upper levels: creatively expressing your own truth, following your dream or bliss, authentic selfhood, melodic voice when speaking and singing, inner strength, self discipline.

Lower levels: addictions, lack of will power, deception and lying, selectively hearing what you want to, creativity with distortions, weak minded.

Sixth Chakra

The *sixth chakra* is the seat of intuition and the intellect. This energy center may be found around the brows and forehead. Weak energy in this area is expressed as mental difficulties. With this energy we experience inner imagery, dreams, fantasies, and higher forms of logic and intuition.

Provides energy to: the brain, pituitary and pineal glands, neurological system, eyes, ears and *nose*

Archetypal principles: intellectual ideas or intuitive capabilities. Images include, mythological creatures like the winged dragon, Pegasus, and the unicorn. Because these creatures represent the higher mind and creative urges, messages received from them bring a broader perspective and creative insights.

Upper levels: telepathy, clairaudience, clairvoyance, intuitive insights, intuitive creativity, higher logic such a philosophy.

Lower levels: fear of intuitive people due to lack of understanding, inability for insights, unaware of intuition, general inability to make use of the innate gifts of this chakra.

Crown Chakra

The *crown chakra* is the seat of the unconscious mind. The perspectives are broad and spiritually refined. It is located at the top (or crown) of the head, a place that allows spiritual consciousness to enter the body. When the crown chakra opens, we have peak experiences that are difficult to tell others because, we don't have concepts for this dimension and it is beyond our ability to express it fully using the lower faculties.

Provides energy to: the entire bodymind. Disruptive energy brings mental, physical, and emotional difficulties. If this energy is healthy, the person will be centered and at peace.

Archetypal principles: unity or oneness with all of creation. Inner images are of light with feeling sensations of love and compassion.

Upper levels: In an open crown chakra experience one finds oneself in a vividly beautiful world where all of the inhabitants are divinely valuable beings. A vale of ignorance has been lifted and there is a feeling that we have a wonderfully divine purpose, Christ consciousness or unity consciousness, harmony and flow, absence of striving.

Lower levels: fear of people who display the consciousness of this chakra, lack of awareness, inability to make use of the gifts of this chakra, misuse of spiritual experiences.

Eighth Chakra

The *eighth chakra* some see as the seat of the soul. It is located out side of the body, just above the crown chakra. Seers have access to the collective past and future and the vast archetypal cosmic influences.

Provides energy to: balance the emotional and spiritual energies, symbolic thought, mental perspectives, open to archetypal forces and innate psychic talents. You have "eyes to see and ears to hear" beyond the mortal materialistic realm.

Archetypal principles: channeling, precognition, balance, equality, sense of the body's connection to the cosmos.

Upper levels: psychic phenomena such as precognition and distance seeing, surrender to what is, fair witnessing, no judgment, awareness with a lack of concern, "in but not of the world," understands synchronicity and lives in a flow of events with faith.

Lower levels: lack of awareness of the higher levels of Self, fear of God, religious delusions.

The chakras are thought to channel a living energy through our bones and flesh. Every traditional culture, whether it be Japanese, Asian, Chinese, Indian, Native American, or Greek, acknowledges this life force that resides in objects as well as living flesh. This force is an endless energy, vast and limitless, a river without beginning or end. The Greeks called this energy *pneuma*: the Asians *prana*, the Japanese *Qi* the Chinese call it as *chi* and the Native Americans refer to it as the Flow of Spirit.

Whatever name you use, it is the flowing of a universal life force from the Creator of the universe to each of us and is seen as the basis of psychological, physical, and spiritual health in virtually every traditional culture. Who can dispute that a life force/energy surrounds and permeates every cell, organ, and sense? As long as the life force flows through our body, all the organs, senses, and systems function optimally. Illness happens when something, psychological or physical, blocks this flow of the life force. Without the freely flowing energy, organs function with less efficiency, blood and lymph flows slow down and waste accumulates contributing to the manifestation of illness of the mind, body, and spirit. When the life force leaves the body, death occurs.

Your way of life will directly affect the quality of the flow of energy that enriches or impoverishes your existence. Practices that strengthen the life force have formed the basis for religious and spiritual life for eons. Art depicting spiritual teachers with a glowing countenance and energy emanating from them abound. For example, in Christianity, Jesus is depicted with a halo around his head.

Turning to another example, the following case study demonstrates the use of the chakra's levels in interpreting meanings behind the symbolic imagery of nighttime dreams and visualizations. We also explored the symbology of the body's symptoms to help clarify areas of a man's life to which he need to bring more psychological and spiritual understanding.

A Case of Arrested Development

When I first met Charles, he was a man in passionate pursuit of the symbolic meanings of his inner imagery. He kept a nightly journal of his dreams and spent several hours each day in meditation during which he witnessed vivid imagery. Intriguingly, he talked about his dreams and meditations as though he had visited other realms of existence. And it was through his meditations that he found symbolic treasures that helped him make sense of his waking life.

During the day, he was a successful dentist, but Charles was not happy. He disliked his traditional practice and longed to do more spiritual counseling. Although he was a virtual hermit and spent much of his time in isolation from others, he intensely sought a grace-filled life. He had the first level of Maslow's pyramid taken care of, and could provide for himself, but his development was somehow blocked.

In the beginning of our time together, Charles's affect was flat, his body overly thin, and his posture which curved forward and sunk at the chest spoke to me of a deep depression. He was emotionally guarded and difficult to talk to. He described himself as "homeless" and seemed to be imprisoned in a body that couldn't adequately express itself to the outside world.

Charles's dream and meditation images indicated that he was searching the upper chakras or the upper spiritual realms of his psyche for relief from the suffering he experienced in the material world. For example: His morning meditations often contained references to the major chakras. One of Charles's meditations went like this: "When I naturally lit up my energy body, my heart was at first painful, as it is wont. I focused upon lighting up my whole body until I could feel it down to my feet. My first and second chakras were not as lit up, whereas my third and fourth chakras were prominently lit up. I felt lucky that there was a crack in the third chakra as I thought it was an escape route to the lower chakras. Otherwise, I would be an entombed mind." He went on to talk about the wealth of the lower chakras "like gold at the bottom of a mine." Then the scene changed and he was standing with a group of homeless derelict men. He said that twice grief came near the surface but he focused upon his heart center and used his meditative breathing to stimulate the heart. In doing this he felt his heart center expand considerably. Just then a blonde woman appeared in his meditation and they began to kiss. As they kissed, Charles said that they were no longer in the physical world but one of floating as if they were weightless. As he ended his meditation he reported, "My heart center moved back towards its more cramped space." He had to return to the material world and its cruel realities.

With his overly thin appearance, long hair, and beard, Charles reminded me of a spiritual renunciate who was living his life in the highly valued upper spiritual chakras and not inhabiting the lower ones. Although his meditation experience indicated that he placed a metaphorically "gold" value on them, during our talk sessions, he spoke of the spiritual realities as if they were the only important part of his life. I knew he was sincere in his quest for spiritual knowledge and I told him that I thought a spiritual journey of this kind might hold promise, but that I held a different perspective. I liked being in the body and found my worldly experience to be just as divine as the energetic or spiritual part of me. Charles listened to my logic and eventually agreed. Together, we discussed how to work on strengthening the energy of his lower three chakras. In other words, how to do the psychological work necessary to heal from past traumas.

We both knew that the lower three chakras provides the archetypal energy that gives personality traits to the ego. We discussed how a healthy ego was a necessary foundation for the divinely important work of the upper chakra realms of Spirit.

Charles listened with interest as I told him: "I saw the kiss of the woman as your yearning for a love connection with a real woman, as well as a yearning for a love connection with the Divine."

He agreed and added, "I also see it as a desire to have a feminine woman in my life, but I also want very much to get in touch with the

Archetypal Growth and Development

higher feminine energies I know I have available to me, but have trouble expressing."

Later, in my office and without Charles present, I did an active imagination meditation and asked for a guide to come forward in my imagination and give Charles instruction about how to heal the lower chakras. Merlin the magician appeared. He stood with outstretched hands, one held towards the heavens and one hand towards the earth in a gesture of greeting. I felt he was also indicating that we should bring the upper and the lower worlds into balance. He said, "The heart chakra is where the two worlds meet. The material world and the Spirit world hold this space in common." Then, I saw a swirling star constellation like the Milky Way. Merlin said, "Tell Charles that we are a part of the All That Is and when you realize who you truly are, you will not feel bad about yourself."

Moving in slow motion, Merlin told me to tell Charles to consider adding more color to his home and thus to his life. The color purple, like Merlin's cape was suggested.

Looking at, wearing, or being exposed to color, whether in the form of light, pigment, or cloth, can affect us at levels we are only just beginning to understand. Who among us has not been emotionally moved by color? Material science tells us that color doesn't exist, and that we see color because of how the sun's rays strike the textures on the object. It is understood that it is our eyes that contain the ability to see colors. Is it possible that color exists as an archetypal energy that cannot be measured by scientific instruments, but can be seen by us?

Then Merlin began moving in slow dramatic gestures. His cape, hair, and beard moved in slow motion, too. From his actions, an idea came to me. I sensed that physical movement like tai chi would help Charles' psyche get back into his body and connect to his lower chakras and to the material world. By his appearance I *knew* that he was not in touch with, and did not value, his body. Movement therapy would be a good choice.

The need to balance the chakras was also perceived by Charles as he reported dreams and meditations in which he saw his energy body. One night, the upper four chakras were lit up, and in his mind's eye, he saw a split or gash just under the fourth chakra or heart center. He thought this was because he felt cut off from his material self. At times, he would symbolically receive instructions for healing himself. For instance, in many dreams he found himself inside of buildings. The building represented his body and he would find himself in the upper part of the building. He reported a knowing that he needed to go downstairs to the lower levels.

To further help you understand what was happening to Charles, he and I often discussed his difficult childhood. His family lived on a Utah farm and his first chakra physical needs were taken care of. However, the family was an emotionally distant one and he never felt loved or emotionally secure, something we all need in order to develop a healthy second chakra energy flow.

During his first year in his dentistry practice, Charles was enjoying the exploration of meditation techniques. His parents, who followed a conservative religion, saw his meditation practices as evil and of the devil. Because his meditation explorations were a threat to their way of thinking, they had him shamefully kidnapped, held for months, and "reprogrammed." Not only did he lose his dentistry practice, but his family forced his live-in girlfriend to flee. Needless to say, this was a blow with disastrous consequences to the energy of his third chakra and his personal power. I felt that this situation had caused an injury to his psyche at the young adult stage and that his earlier childhood development may have also been adversely affected by his family of origin. Although he would move miles away from his family, it would take years for him to recover.

Charles and I used the chakra system as an assessment tool to give useful information about where he most needed to work through his issues to regain a physical, psychological, and spiritual balance in his life. As he worked through the issues of the chakras involved, Charles grew in self-awareness and moved in a positive way through his developmental tasks. During our work together, he came to understand that it was part of his spiritual path to learn to love the manifest world and himself as a part of it. Eventually, he came to love his body in the world, and in doing so, his spiritual nature deepened.

Today and years after our first meeting, his developmental tasks are nearly complete; he is a person who functions as well in his lower material chakras as in his upper chakra's spiritual energy. Charles's ego needs are being satisfied and a healthy self-esteem has been established. He has developed beyond the injured personal self to a true feeling of community and loving kindness towards others. He is truly a self-actualizing person on a grace-filled path.

With clients, I patiently listen and watch for clues of what she/he may need. I set a few basic goals, suspend judgment, and then work spontaneously taking action, like offering insight producing tools in the moment. I set my intentions and allow Nature to take its course. Synchronicity, or meaningful consequences, happens during therapy that facilitates client growth. When these instances occur,

Archetypal Growth and Development

I take it as an indication that our timing and intentions are in line with the client's natural course. If all goes well, their development is completed in a positive way; their consciousness is raised and they experience an ego expansion or development to the next stage of their growth.

Each of us has the potential to recognize the mysteries buried in our soul and as we learn to explore the symbology of our body's symptoms, the knowledge will help clarify areas of our life into which we need to bring more psychological and spiritual understanding. Tools that use an archetypal psychology help us retrieve unconscious information and grant us insights on how to best live our life. With each new insight, the soul shines through a little more and we grow, each according to an innate timing known only to our earthly bodies and our spiritual Nature. The Greek philosophers named this innate call to growth, *physis*.

Chapter 4
Health as Expanding Consciousness

At Dawn the Lotus Opens its Petals to the Day

As a transpersonal counselor with training in the healing arts, I make use of archetypal images and levels of consciousness in the imagination. Healing arts such as dream interpretation, guided imagery, astrology, Tarot counseling, and many forms of artistic expression are tools that are used to reveal hidden symbolic meanings in client health issues.

Many counselors understand that clients come to therapeutic resolution quicker when healing arts techniques and symbology are integrated with talk therapy. In my experience, people are most receptive to psychological intervention when they are in crisis. The heightened awareness that the thought of death or disability brings, offers clients a chance to see illness, injury, and other difficulties as obstacles that have come into their life as *divine challenges.* Working with their challenge, the counselor helps them through difficult experiences, which moves them forward in their development and closer to their full potential. When they make the commitment to begin this type of work, they quickly learn to view their medical situation from entirely new perspectives.

Let's put it another way. Defining behavioral patterns in clients' personalities in terms of the archetypes is a perspective that is used in illness, injury, and difficult life situations. The crisis gives people the opportunity to become more aware and as they gain awareness, they work through life's lessons, growing into the next level of their development. The evolving life patterns contain the *urge* towards wholeness of self. The challenges are seeded with opportunities to gain insights and grow toward self-actualization, individuation, and enlightenment.

Psychological health is attained by becoming more conscious of the major dysfunctional patterns in the personality. To help our clients, we need to know how they react to certain environments, like the hospital, family systems, and the community. Using their health crisis as a catalyst, clients learn to identify unhealthy patterns of behavior that may have contributed to the present problems. An experienced counselor helps them gain insights, or new ideas about their situation, that are needed for optimal psychological and physical healing to occur.

The following story is an example of a session in which the creative process helped a client see dysfunctional life patterns. This story is a common one of a man who is trying to be an archetypal warrior and handle a difficult situation by himself.

A Case of the Hiccups

Forty-year-old Nelson was in the hospital for heart surgery. He had been a client for some time but, in the past, his issues had more to do with relationship woes than physical symptoms. Nevertheless, here we were, the surgery had corrected the problem and he was expected to do well. After the surgery, he experienced a severe case of hiccups. He suffered four days with continuous hiccups. Apparently, the hospital staff had tried various treatments but nothing worked. He finally called and asked for a healing arts session in his hospital room.

Luckily, I thought to bring my husband, Lewis, to guard the door so that we wouldn't be disturbed during the session. As it turned out, there were three potential interruptions that may have affected the outcome of treatment. One nurse asked my husband what going on in the room. When he told her it was a "healing session," she walked away dismissively stating, "What-ev-er."

Nelson was lying in his hospital bed hiccupping hard. My first impression was that he was sobbing. Because he was of the "boys don't cry" generation, I felt that Nelson *was* symbolically sobbing his heart out in the only way that he could.

Because Nelson's condition was life threatening, he had been confined to the hospital bed for several days. He was in crisis and afraid that he might die. This anxious emotional state of arousal caused him to contemplate upon his life at deeper levels. However,

Health as Expanding Consciousness

he was being a good soldier, like our culture taught, and holding emotions in check. Because of his macho mindset, he couldn't express emotions freely and so his body had to produce an archetypal pattern of behavior that would express that kind of energy. As he held onto his anxiety, his body symbolically expressed his fear and anxiety through hiccups.

The intervention began when he saw me come into the room. Before I entered, I had centered myself in my spirituality and embodied the healer archetype. This centeredness played a part in the healing because, at some level, he recognized the spiritual space I was in and, during the course of treatment, caught the "high." This interpenetration of energy between the healer and the healee would move his consciousness towards his own high. The phenomenon of a *contact high* facilitates psychological movement and is an important factor in healing.

With his permission, I approached his bed to begin treatment. My education and intuition told me to place my hand on his diaphragm to begin an archetypal energy work. I silently said a quick prayer for protection and asked for healing energy. (Because of my receptive state of mind, I sometimes take on a mild form of the client's symptoms. I find asking for protection, at the same time that I ask for healing energy, prevents this transference.) As I placed my hand in the area of his fourth chakra, he anxiously grabbed my arm with both hands; like the action of someone grabbing a lifeline. I was startled, but stayed calm and directed him to just close his eyes and rest.

My intention was to cure his hiccups by starting the process with energy work and then to allow the patterns to unfold. Whatever they were, I didn't know. After that I would choose, in the moment, the best healing arts tool for the situation. The evolving archetypal patterns can't be predicted ahead of time or explained with logic because the patterns are unpredictable and unique to each person. The unfolding of life patterns are experienced in the immediacy of the moment and are clearer in retrospect.

Standing by his bed, with warm healing energy running through my hand, like water from a hose, I placed my hand on his diaphragm and then remained quiet. After a few minutes, his facial expression signaled relaxation and a meditative level of consciousness. I confidently and quietly explained, "We are going to use your imagination to cure your hiccups." I directed him to take his consciousness inside his body and down to the area of his hiccups. He was instructed to allow an image to form of his hiccups.

After a moment and still in meditation, he said, "I see a piece of rope that is twisted up at the end." I asked him what needed to happen, and he said, "The rope needs to untwist so I can relax."

I guided him to allow the rope to unwind and suggested that his body relax as he visualized the rope untwisting. After about a minute, I directed him to draw in healing energy with the "in" breath and on the "out" breath to expel negative energy in all its forms: thoughts, feelings, and images. Speaking quietly, I drew his attention to the feeling aspect of the body relaxing and the letting go of tension.

The hiccups slowly subsided. After the imagery session, I talked to him about how men in our culture are not taught to manage their emotions. I briefly told him about his feminine side and gave him the suggestion that he honor this aspect more fully and learn to express himself as a fully sensitive male.

After thirty minutes of energy work, guided imagery, and verbal counseling, my client was again in charge of his emotions and we had worked out a plan: Pray about how to allow sensitive emotions to find expression naturally.

Two days later, I heard, through a friend, that Nelson was suffering a reoccurrence of the hiccups. I figured he was "toughing it out" and didn't want to call me. So I called him. Because his teenage son was present in his room, I briefly gave Nelson an assignment. When he was alone, he was to write down a list of things that he was afraid of, to say a short prayer for guidance, and wait in meditation for answers. Throughout this time he was to allow his emotions to come naturally.

During phone counseling, he calmed down but still had light hiccups. Later in the evening he was able to cure his hiccups by using the techniques of emotional release I taught him over the phone. Nelson later reported, "I closed my eyes to pray, and during my meditation, the dam broke and I cried like a baby."

Hiccup free, Nelson called the next day and reported that he felt emotionally centered. Because of this emotional crisis, he was convinced that he needed to work on his emotional self and was looking forward to learning how to express his archetypal feminine side. "I don't want to hold onto my emotions so much that they have to be expressed as bodily problems." He continued, "This makes me see that if I don't try harder to understand myself in relation to my wife, I will die."

In this example, diagnosis, and treatment of his heart condition was left to medical science. I intellectually assessed the underlying archetypal pattern of the whole person, intuition followed and

Health as Expanding Consciousness

an artistic process using a few healing arts was set in motion. His awareness of the other dimensions of himself expanded and he learned that he needed to make changes in ways that handled his emotions. This challenge was successfully completed, the lessons learned, and the hiccups disappeared.

Consciousness Development

Consciousness must be accounted for in all descriptions of reality. Beneath and beyond the brain's anatomical and chemical strata, there is a level on which consciousness is the primary force. Many hypotheses have been written about the quantum brain and the holographic mind, but what concerns us here is how our conscious knowing is supported by those around us: family, community and our institutions.

The primary function of a family is to interpret and edit society's codes of conduct and communicate them to their children. Our life's lessons begin in infancy and much of these early lesson's content is subliminal i.e., eye contact, facial expression, hand gestures, expressive voice tones and a sense of personal space. Every infant is born with a blueprint for life in the brain, physically, mentally, and spiritually. We are uniquely equipped with a repertoire of behaviors adapted to the environment in which we evolve. This repertoire is dependent on innate mechanisms in the central nervous system and that become activated when appropriate stimuli are encountered in the environment. This means that when your family interacts with the newborn, large shares of your family's interactive traits are imprinted in its brain. Metaphorically, the infant is like a copy machine.

First, let's look at archetypal traits of the upper refined levels and the lower primitive levels (discussed in Chapter 3). Reality is much more complex but this two-level division is easy to work with in a transpersonal or wellness counseling situation.

At the primitive levels: If your parents had a predominately dysfunctional pattern, you unconsciously take on some of the dysfunction. You can't help it. The family imprints your brain so that you think, feel, see, and love according to the life patterns that get passed down through the generations. Some take most of their life to heal the dysfunction—if they do heal. If the family's inherited traits are grossly negative, it could take a lifetime to traverse the challenges and clean up the family's emotional inheritance— if they worked on it. Many do not know how to work on their issues and, at this time in medicine, clients do not receive wellness or transpersonal care.

At the more refined levels: Generally speaking, a child raised by parents that had few challenges would have few challenges him/herself. If the family was psychologically stable, the children would be imprinted with that stability. The child develops a strong sense of self or strong ego. He has concepts for prevailing norms but also gains a more important insight—that the rules of society are, for the most part, only relative and he can abandon some of these values if they do not fit his *true self.* However, even if the family is of a more positive emotional inheritance, of the upper more positive levels of the archetypes, there can be other types of challenges. For example, sometimes people raised in a positive environment see themselves as a standard for "normal." (I call these people *normals.*) Basically, because of their stability, everything works for them and other people should "be able to do things the way I do." They can be critical and judgmental of others. This is one of the most difficult family imprints to work with because they aren't uncomfortable and they feel righteous in their thinking.

In any family, there is a cast of archetypal characters, mothers, fathers, siblings, and grandparents. The larger communities of schools and social organizations have certain types of characters and ditto the larger community of the world. How we are treated in that original family and our society contributes to our internal world and effects self-acceptance and self-esteem.

Whatever our situation, it is our particular life's path. From a developmental perspective, our suffering and challenges are obstacles for us to overcome. The effort it takes to get over our challenges—at the mental, spiritual, and physical levels—pushes one forward on an archetypal expansive growth pattern that includes healing.

During the healing/growing experience, there is a shift in the psyche, and something occurs to the healee that was not apparent before. In a moment of insight, the healee gets an *ah-ha* sense and an answer or direction occurs to them. Once the healee receives the message of the challenge, he or she grows in awareness and the individual's consciousness is expanded.

Whatever the course, bottom line, it is the counselor's responsibility to understand the family and cultural situation of the person so that they have a holistic picture of who their client is. This doesn't have to be a long information gathering session all at once, but can be gathered throughout the counseling relationship with them.

While the traditional medical model tends to confine illness to an emphasis on pathology, nurse theorist Margaret Newman suggests that the way to health is to recognize dysfunctional patterns and provide opportunities for insight that opens new pathways in the brain. This encourages those in our care to raise their consciousness and learn new ways of coping.

We are at the dawning of a more balanced system of healing. We observe the yin and yang coming together in each of us and our environments; a balance of the masculine linear and feminine intuitive—major archetypal principles. At this time in health care, we bear witness to evolutionary leaps towards more holistic methods in healing.

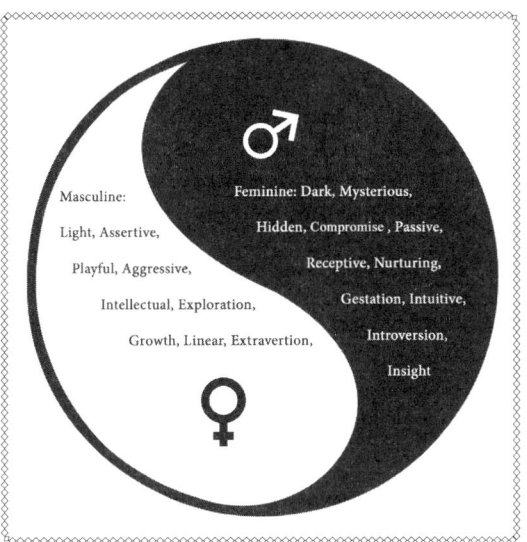

Yin and Yang

The traditional medical paradigm expects predictable and fixable outcomes to disease and injury. The healing artist focuses on the whole person within the context of his or her family and community. Health is seen as the evolving whole, rather than focused upon the individual's disease. With this new focus, intuition plays a larger role. The intuitive healer, with training in the healing arts, views the whole person, offers assessments, and then acts as a guide in the creative healing process towards health. With this process, the outcomes vary according to the needs, readiness, and ability of the client to gain insights and move toward health. And the payoff is this: As you engage in this work, you bear witness to a magnificent magical and spirit-filled world that creatively and developmentally strives toward an expanded consciousness—toward health of the mind, body, and the spirit.

Chapter Five
Archetypes of the Community

Differing Spectrums of Light in the Same Rainbow

During the writing of an emotional story about friends, I had a peak experience that raised my consciousness. It lasted for about as long as it takes lightening to light up a darkened sky. As this mystical experience illuminated the landscape of my inner world, I saw images of my family and friends. In that brief moment, I *knew* that all people everywhere were incredibly beautiful, part of something that is awesome and that embraces both suffering and healing. I also understood that with our limited central nervous system, we can never comprehend the entire picture and this tiny peek was beyond my ordinary reality.

Through these types of experiences, I have come to understand that our minds are limited. Thus we must be cautious of our judgments. As far as I can tell, if we exist, then everyone and everything should be respected as coming from a divine source. Clearly, the levels of the archetype are available to us or we wouldn't recognize them. And so it would make sense that during counseling situations—indeed any conversation—we must endeavor to think dynamically and holistically while keeping an open and receptive mind. Remember: We are working with a multi-dimensional person who has a rich tapestry of interpersonal relationships in which many archetypes operate.

Circumstances in our lives prompt emergence of certain archetypal roles, and within theses roles, multiple levels of expression exist. Archetypal energies are dynamic and fluctuate according to our actions, our thoughts, our emotions and our intentions. Because we may consciously choose the level in which we live our lives, moment to moment, our aim should be to make every action a higher action, every thought a higher thought, and every intention a higher intention.

> ### Archetypes of the Unconscious and Collective Unconscious
>
> The unconscious mind is a personal reservoir of experience unique to each individual. It is the structure of the psyche that autonomously organizes personal experience. The collective unconscious is a part of the unconscious mind—a universal and impersonal nature which is identical in all individuals. The collective unconscious accumulates and organizes personal experiences in similar ways, but it does not develop individually. Rather, it is inherited, consisting of pre-existent energies known as archetypes.

Archetypes in the Big Picture

Years of community activism have given me an opportunity to view the archetypal patterns in the social system of my small town. In contrasting characters in my community with characters on television commentaries and news broadcasts, I could see similar human traits in other places. In fact, I have come to see that all communities have a rich tapestry of archetypal characters that can be found around the world and throughout the centuries. The names of these patterns differ from culture to culture, but the essences of the archetypes are universal.

In this chapter, we will identify four major archetypes in a typical community. We call these four archetypes *fundamentalist*, *conservative*, *liberal*, and *spiritualist* and we can embody all four archetypes, at different times. Our values, and the way we chose to live our life, dictates which is the predominate expression. In other words, our choice in values affects our intentions, our thinking, and our actions, thus defining which archetypes dominate.

The following archetypal perspectives are but a thin slice of peoples' lives—a small sampling of group consciousness in the bigger picture.

Archetypal Fundamentalist

The *archetypal fundamentalist* perspective is not restricted to the religious, but can include any people who act in primitive or basic ways such as the street gangs, politicians, or the police. The fundamentalist way of thinking is concrete black and white; issues are either right or wrong.

At the lower levels, we see ourselves as more right or more pious and everyone else as wrong. Thus, a dogmatic "us versus them" perspective prevails. The fundamentalist may feel misunderstood or outcast by the mainstream and this may stimulate idealism to a point of aggression or even fanaticism. Indeed, a suspicion toward higher education may exist when fundamentalistic ideals blind us to seeing larger patterns and dimensions in the world. Those embodying this archetype are often seen by others as limited in their ability to think critically, which often leads toward the dismissal of anyone who thinks or feels differently. If we become too immersed in our fundamentalistic attitudes (and current neuroscience has demonstrated that we all have unconscious fundamentalistic biases), we will tend to cling to stubborn, entrenched positions that defy reasoned argument or contradictory evidence. Fundamentalism, from the perspective of cognitive psychology, limits our ability to be self-aware of ourselves, of others, and of society as a whole. It can bias our selection of work and friends, and such biases have the propensity to generate unconscious hostility and aggression.

Fundamentalist thinking causes us to hold onto old ideas. For example, old patriarchal rules might dominate over contemporary issues of women's rights and human rights. At the extreme levels, fundamentalist communities may choose to isolate themselves from society, and within these groups, individual expression may be limited.

At a higher level, fundamentalism, in and of itself, does not necessarily lead to anti-social behavior. Actually, the research suggests that only a very small percentage of fundamentalists take hostile actions toward others. In fact, the vast majority generates profound kindness and charity toward others, and it is only the fringe element that captures the attention of the media. The main theme of fundamentalism seems to be more about experiencing and not about critical thinking.

Archetypal Conservatives

For the *archetypal conservatives*, values cannot be accounted for according to age or generation. Conservatism is more of a lifestyle that is not limited to political or religious views.

At the lower levels, we maintain traditional relationships and conventional religious beliefs with a masculine dominance. We tend to live with a set of beliefs that offer us certainty, and we may play it safe by not supporting progressive agendas that challenge traditional values.

At the upper levels, the conservative can be seen as one who prefers to preserve a traditional way of life. We are moderately idealistic and see helping others both as a duty and a pleasure. Conservatives are not risk-takers, are cautiously moderate, and have an approach that is steady and middle-of-the-road.

Archetypal Liberal

The *archetypal liberal* is basically a free thinker—an open-minded individual who values his/her freedom of choice.

At the lower levels, he/she may be an elitist and choose a shallow viewpoint in religion and politics and promote it with out knowing all the details and ramifications. A propensity to exhibit impulsiveness and make decisions without thinking things through may prevail. We may follow but do not feel bound by traditional or conventional standards, and because of that, our lifestyle may be unconventional.

At the upper levels, some liberals may choose a traditional lifestyle, but they do not look to restrict others' choices. They are tolerant on all fronts and favor progress or reform in political and religious affairs. They tend to fight against prejudice and bigotry, but, as I mentioned before, can just as easily be blind to their own conservative and fundamentalist biases. They espouse openness, tolerance, and compassion toward everyone, and emphasize receptiveness to others' ideas. They often favor innovation and progress and do best in jobs that have the opportunity for creativity. A large proportion of artists tend to be liberal, and self-actualization is a commonly sought-after goal.

Archetypal Spiritualist

The *archetypal spiritualist* includes the self-actualizing individual inclined towards mysticism. Their main goal in life is to live a Grace-filled life. They may study one or more wisdom traditions but may not follow the tenets of the system/s to the letter. In other words, when we operate at this level, we consciously choose what to believe moment by moment depending upon the circumstance. At this level we are comfortable with ambiguity.

At the lower levels, we are thrown back into lower level fundamentalism or, at best, can only achieve Grace at intervals and have yet to develop the ability to maintain the pattern. In other words, we can talk the talk, but fall down repeatedly while learning to walk the walk.

At the higher levels of the spiritualist archetype, we have a cosmic view that is broad and inclusive. We might have extraordinary talents such as highly developed psychic abilities and the ability to heal the sick. We consciously strive to be non-judgmental and to be the best we can be at all times.

Each archetypal perspective has its own take on the world and is a level of consciousness that brings contributions to the table of life. Because they exist across time and in all cultures, these perspectives are a part of the All That Is. Although they have coexisted uncomfortably for eons, each of the archetypal values is here to stay. In a positive light, we may see them as serving a bigger purpose. In the bigger picture, we can see them holding the whole together in a tension that prevents extremes from forming in any one perspective.

From a developmental perspective, one can see a pattern emerging from the fundamental mind, to the conservative mindset to the more liberal and finally the mature spiritualist. Each major archetype can be seen as a stage of human development that is expressing itself in groups. For instance, broadly speaking, the fundamentalist's consciousness is like a youth or an adolescent. The conservative view is more in keeping with young to middle-adulthood and the liberal perspective is middle adulthood to elder and at the highest level, the spiritualist, reflects a higher self-actualizing mind. Remember that these stages are dynamic in all of us and we choose which level to operate in moment to moment. However, it takes a practiced self-awareness to predominately operate in the higher levels of the archetypes.

Again, with all the respectable research available about life after death, one must consider the perspective of reincarnation. (We discuss this in more detail in Chapter 6.) Borrowing from that perspective, one might go through these cultural growth stages in one lifetime or take several lifetimes to move through the learning of one of these societal developmental levels.

Now, lets go back to the subject of expanding consciousness and show how knowledge of these three major archetypes help the counselor guide another in their healing journey. The following story involves one man's struggle against the forces of prejudice and the archetypes that carry that way of thinking.

Reflections of the Whole Person

Nathan, a 52-year-old African-American man, came seeking help in order to cope with a diagnosis of prostate cancer. He wanted to learn all he could about how the mind affects the body and use that knowledge in his treatment. He was a highly intellectual professional man but he had lost touch with how to treat his body. Consequently, when cancer struck, he had to catch up on the latest nutritional, and mind-body theories. I also taught him how his disease could give us information and help him grow developmentally.

Nathan often expressed anger regarding racial issues, which also had to do with his masculine place in society. He entered conflicts whenever he could. Consequently, he had channeled the archetype of anger through his body at the lower chakras for extended periods.

Anger is an archetype associated with the ego or lower chakras and, as I saw it, the anger disrupted the natural energy flow and the target area of the prostate was paying the price. Because I see disease as a meaningful reflection of the whole person, we talked about these symbolic implications and decided that his anger was an important topic of discussion for this session.

Nathan was a fan of Barack Obama, so I took this occasion to contrast his personality with Obama's. In my assessment, Nathan needed to see where anger fit in as a level of consciousness. I asked him, "Did you see the movie, called *Troy*, where Brad Pitt plays Achilles?"

Nathan set up straight, smiled, and said, "Yeah, that is one of my favorite movies."

Next, I asked him to recall the last scene of the movie where Achilles, after a lifetime of fighting, was dying. "As the camera pans away from Achilles on his death bed, you can see warriors fighting on all sides of him." I told Nathan, "Anger and fighting is archetypal. There has always been anger and, because of the differing perspectives in the world, there will always be something to fight about." I paused to see if he was following. He nodded and I continued, "At some point, in your life, you have to see that anger is harmful and give up fighting." Giving him an example, I said, "Do you notice how Obama doesn't get angry publicly? He seems very Zen master-like."

"Yeah," Nathan said, and then asked, "What is a Zen master?"

At first, I wondered how to quickly explain, just what a Zen master was and not miss a beat with this session's goal. After a moment, it came to me that a model of consciousness would work to demonstrate this complicated transpersonal concept. On a sheet of paper, I drew a large circle and told him, "This is the level of the ego." Second, I drew a smaller circle inside of the larger circle and labeled it "soul." I pointed to the smaller circle inside and talked about the attributes of the soul as being a calm detached observer and taking things in stride. At the

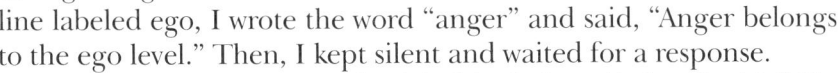

line labeled ego, I wrote the word "anger" and said, "Anger belongs to the ego level." Then, I kept silent and waited for a response.

Nathan looked at me, sat back in his chair, smiled and said, "Oh, Okay."

In that moment, I *knew* that Nathan had received an *ah-ha* moment of clarity and insight. He now had a rudimentary knowledge of a Zen master and a better idea of the level of consciousness that his anger was coming from. Our conversation continued.

Nathan was an archetypal warrior with a highly developed intuition and personal value system. In his own way, for the last twenty-five or thirty years, he had taken it upon himself to change people's perspectives of blacks in America. However, while on this mission, he was in a mental and emotional fray with people he didn't really like, especially those who held different perspectives and beliefs.

Over the course of our conversation, Nathan came to understand that his anger was hurting his body and, if he wanted to be healthy, his fighting days were over. I suggested that he try a more peaceful lifestyle, one with time for prayer and meditation. Most of all, he was to avoid the people who brought out his anger. Because of his predominantly liberal archetype, he was always fighting the fundamentalist and the conservative perspectives, an ancient fight that would not be resolved. To further his healing, I suggested that he surround himself with family and friends who wished him well and with whom he felt accepted and loved.

As you can see, it behooves the counselor to know the cultural context in which the client lives because it gives clues to the direction that you want to move their consciousness. An aware counselor has a good understanding of the family and cultural systems that clients are embedded in. They use this knowledge to better facilitate client growth and development and help birth their consciousness into the next level of reality.

Chapter 6
Archetypes and Patterns of the Archetypes

*Gracefully, Organizing Patterns
Move Through Our Living*

Psychology is a field that takes into consideration the individual experience and is not just philosophical theories. Medicine recognizes that the human psychological conditions are complex and can be fully grasped only through descriptions based on an individual's case material. In other words, we cannot fit every person's mental and emotional traits into a box of theoretical concepts. In the same way, the person's needs do not end at the physiological. As in the case of the hiccups (in Chapter 3), as we observe each individual scientifically, we also have to consider manifestations of the psyche in its totality. Thoughtful considerations of the individual's life story are essential when considering the whole person. In this chapter we will explore a few larger archetypes that are found abundantly in the material world and in our experiences.

Feminine and Masculine Patterns

The feminine and masculine are broad concepts of related psychic phenomena and physical characteristics. Important to everyone's life story are patterns of the feminine, or anima and the masculine, or animus. The feminine and masculine nature in all of us manifests a life of its own and reacts to influences coming from every field of human experience. These two large energies show themselves in the personal, instinctual, and social spheres as well as in the physical world of shape and direction. Altogether, if we want to understand the psyche, we have to look at the entire world of experience.

In the world of form, the masculine can be seen as a symbol of phallic assertiveness; the multi-storied sky scrapers exemplify such forms. The feminine principle is represented as round, soft shapes and open interior spaces. The spherical shapes found on Russian Cathedrals capture this essence. A knife is masculine and the bowl is feminine. If you look around the environment that you are in, you'll identify many objects that fall into these archetypal realms.

In Nature, the natural growth of plants represents an outgoing masculine principle. The feminine in nature is the waiting period or gestation in the life of a seed. Taking it a bit further, the masculine principle is the force that bursts life from the seed and pushes it to grow. The feminine principle is the waiting bud, and then the bloom holding and nurturing her seeds protecting them, until maturity, for the coming year. Nature's eternal talents mix up the two energies to give us a wholesome show bursting forth with colorful and creative plants and flowers.

In the Cosmos, the sun actively radiates outwardly in a masculine force. The feminine is seen in the moon's passive reflection of the sun's light.

Because we are a part of Nature's dance, the masculine and feminine archetypes express easily recognizable traits. Ideally, the person learns to access a balance of masculine and feminine principle operating in them and find ways to align these two major energies to achieve centeredness and individuation, psychological factors necessary for self-actualization.

The masculine archetypal principle (*animus*) is an energetic force that has an assertive and outgoing nature. Higher-level attributes include assertiveness, building form and structure, exploration, logic, problem-solving abilities, leadership, and fatherly love. At the lower level, the attributes include aggression, stubbornness, lack of responsibility, rigidity, and prejudice.

The feminine archetypal principle (*anima*) is an energetic force that has characteristics of a more passive and introversive nature. The higher-level attributes include receptivity, receiving insights and inspiration, gestation, intuition, love, nurturance, loving mother and so on. At the lower levels, the attributes include fear of the unknown, withholding, passive aggressiveness, and emotional frigidity.

We find the masculine and feminine universal principles in every culture's art and mythology. These two archetypes can be seen as large because they manifest in shape, force, in animal and human expressions, and in everything in our world. For example the spoon has a phallic shaped handle and a feminine oval, the mother bear nurtures her cubs, and a young man sets out on an adventure. These universal principles have been described by philosophers and sages in diverse cultural traditions throughout time. A century ago, anthropologist Claude Levi-Strauss, wrote extensively on the law of opposites. He claimed that in order for a culture to survive, it must cultivate knowledge of and sensitivity for maintaining balance and respecting the masculine and feminine laws of nature. The Chinese traditional philosophy includes Yang (masculine) and Yin (feminine). When we realize how huge these energies are, we must conclude that our imagination contains, and is bound to, these large patterns. In fact, we are bound so firmly that we will project and act them out again and again, at all times and in all places.

The most obvious projections are our mother and father figures. When working with clients, one can tell a great deal about the balance of masculine and feminine energies by talking to them about their early parenting or simply consciously observing how they manifest the masculine and feminine. If, for instance, a man tells you that his mother (or mother figure) was nurturing, he may have a healthy feminine. If he complains that he doesn't feel much empathy for others, therein lays the quality of his inner feminine nature. What people say about their parents, should be a guide to the therapeutic work that needs to be done in order to achieve a balance of the divine pair within.

The Narcissistic Archetypal Patterns

Narcissism is the archetypal principle of self-love. The Creator fashioned us to be aware of ourselves because we need to eat, drink, brush our teeth, comb our hair, and so on. Our narcissism enables us to take care of the whole self: our mind, our body, and our spiritual selves. Interestingly, how we care for our body, tells others how we are doing. The less we like ourselves, the less we care for the body or we overcompensate and become perfectionistic. Our cleanliness routine and clothing style is a direct reflection, the symbolic representation of the level of love of one's self, and of the Self.

The small self is the ego with its cast of easily recognizable roles and archetypal scenarios. The Self is that observer or fair witnessing part of ourselves and is the wiser part of our nature. At the Self level of the archetype, we are better at choosing graceful behavior, even at an early age. Keep in mind that we are also capable of fluctuating up and down the archetypal continuum depending upon ego strength, internal thoughts, and external circumstances. So, the more aware we are of our foibles the better chance we have of advancing up the developmental latter gracefully.

Many of us experienced an injury to the sense of self in the formative years; we know this as the *narcissistic injury*. An example of this injury might be something like a parental abandonment that the small self was unable to contemplate and integrate into the personal story in positive fashion. The injury festers and activates a compensatory mechanism within the self and the person feels compelled to achieve or misbehave in order to compensate for a lack of love.

At the lower levels of the narcissistic archetype, we display the personality traits of vanity, conceit, and selfishness and we look to the exterior world to get the love that we don't have for ourselves. For whatever reason, some people seem destined to remain at this level for a part of their life and others spend whole lives searching "out there" for love. If we are on the healthier path, after a few youthful challenges, we mature and begin to notice others' needs and willingly take on more adult responsibilities. We advance to a higher level and to a healthier level of narcissism or self-love.

With healthy narcissism, the self/ego diminishes and allows the authenticity of the Higher Self to shine through. Healthy narcissists are aware of other's needs and exhibit a strong code of personal and social values in their dealings with others. They, set realistic goals for themselves and have the kind of self-love that allows them to do great things. This has to be the case with many of our authentic and positive role models or we would never have heard from them.

Healthy Narcissism Levels Based Upon Maslow's Hierarchy of Needs Model

Nous/Mind	Soma/Body	Philia/Love
5. cosmic consciousness, omniscience, wisdom	vehicle for the Holy Spirit	Holy Spirit; Cosmic/Self-love
4. insight, reason, understanding	Self-nurturing	Unconditional love; Altruism
3. logic, planning, cooperation	Territorial; Need for boundaries	Self-esteem; Friendship
2. linear thinking, curiosity, creativity	Earthly pleasures, materialism	Relationships, dependency
1. inner senses directed at objects, imprinting	Primitive instincts for survival	Symbiosis, bonding, sexual urges

Identifying the Archetypes and Archetypal Scenarios

As the sequence of events play out in our daily lives, the thinking, feeling, and the interplay between people contain story patterns, or archetypal scenarios, that have played out since the beginning of time. For example, the archetypal scenario of *creating something useful* has been played out in a multitude of ways throughout the centuries. Discoveries are brought into being during these scenarios. *Sharing with others* is another one that goes on day after day with family and friends. The simple act of *playing with others* serves us our entire life. *Healing the wound* is another scenario as is *fighting with others* and *trying to control the situation*.

After studying archetypal patterns for several years, it appears as though everything at its foundation is archetypal: creatures, shapes (sacred geometry), animals' traits, our body shapes, weather patterns, growth patterns in plants, growth and development in people, and so on. With this perspective, our entire cosmos is archetypal. Is that perception formed in our brains and we project what we see? Does the energy of consciousness contain the information of the archetypes? We don't know. At this time, science has no concrete explanation for the archetypes or of consciousness.

From a mystical point of view, the universe can look unified as if everything was made from one creative "mind." It appears as though we are in this space and time to play out the archetypes during our human dramas. However, we must keep in mind that our perceptual abilities are limited. Looking at our everyday living, it seems that we choose archetypal patterns (healer, mystic, scientist, religious person) to become and to believe in. At the same time, because of our ability for self-awareness, we must maintain that self-awareness and practice keeping an open mind. This means that we should not allow our "beliefs" to snap into ridged systems derived on our own, or of a more traditional persuasion.

When I counsel others, I keep my mind as neutral as possible and make use of several intuitive arts such as energy work, guided imagery, Tarot, astrology, and others. In a session, I concentrate on the major human archetypes as my primary map. Since there is a multitude of archetypal information available to me at any one time, it is not possible to label everything. Besides, by the time we feel the qualities of the archetypes, they are already in expression mode within us, mixing it up with our personal and cultural stuff.

Let us take a look at a counseling session in which I will identify some (not all) of the larger archetypes and archetypal scenarios by placing them in italics. Always keep in mind that when we speak of "things" as archetypal, the things are really the "expression" of formless archetypal energy. Read through the following case story, and then go back and practice concentrating within and sense or feel the essence of the archetypes italicized.

> Judy, a 54 year-old *therapist* came to my office with physical *pain* and *anxiety* that was related to an upcoming surgery. She also felt a *depression that was related to life changes*.
>
> Judy *complained* of sciatica down the *back* of her left leg and into her foot. She *described* the pain in her leg as being so *sharp* she couldn't *rest* it on the chair. Her *traditional physician* had *ordered* the usual *diagnostic tests* and thought that the condition might require surgery. She complained of a tightness in her throat that made it difficult to swallow but an examination failed to find a physical cause.
>
> Because *body language* and its disease *symptoms* are *expressions* of the archetypes that are *operating* in the person, Judy and I *explored* the *symbolism* of the affected areas. "The spine is symbolic of *courage*," I said. Since she had *trouble with courage*, I thought she was *operating in the lower levels of the archetypes* and her body was *expressing distress over a lack of courage*. Trouble in the throat chakra area might mean that she was having *difficulty speaking her truth*, as well as a *lack of will to carry out that truth*.
>
> Judy was *familiar* with the chakra system. She thought, "The problem with the spinal cord in the area of the second chakra probably had to do with *not working with the right group of people* because I *feel alone* in the office." She mentioned that she would like to *change* her *profession* and do something more *meaningful* with her life.
>
> Since the *second* issue was of less importance than the *pain* and *anxiety* about her surgery, the focus of the *first* session was to *decrease* these presenting symptoms. After actively *listening* to Judy *verbalize* her *fears*, anxieties and possible career changes, I moved the *conversation* back to her physical and emotional pain and suggested a guided imagery session.
>
> After a *brief relaxation phase*, I had her go to a *special place* in her *imagination*. With her *inner eye*, she described a *peaceful scene* under an apple *tree*. Next, I asked her to find an image to represent her pain.

Looking at her *inner* body, she said, "The pain is a light in a *strait line* down my spine and leg *culminating* in a bunch of *sparks* at my foot." I told her to "*breathe* in *healing energy* in a healing color and send it to the site of the pain and on the out breath, blow out pain and anxiety." She did this for several minutes as I *occasionally* coached her. After a *short time*, she *reported* that, in her imagination, a deer was there and had begun to gently *nuzzle* her neck. Judy felt that he was a *healing* deer and was there to remove the pain.

My *intention* was to *teach* her a guided imagery *exercise* that was *effective* in *decreasing* pain that she could *use on her own*. The technique made use of the images of the imagination to see energy and utilized the breath to focus the *attention* to move healing energy through the body and *disperse* any energy *blockages* that contributed to her pain. In this case, it *stimulated* her imagination to bring in an image of a deer with an archetypal *gentleness* that aided the healing.

At the end of the imagery session, she told me the light in the line of her leg had *faded*, the sparks were gone and the pain had *eased*. When she was *finished*, and *returned to full consciousness*, I instructed her to *practice* the imagery at least *once* a day and to return in *one* week.

The following week, Judy reported that the imagery helped relieve the pain and she felt more *peaceful*. She *abruptly* began talking about her career change. I understood that it was time to delve into this issue using synchronicity and the archetypes of Tarot cards. She chose the Paladini deck and asked the question, "*What do I need to know to get better?*"

After Judy's question and shuffle, she drew the first of five cards. I use a projective technique with the cards and only read the cards after the client has made his/her own associations (more about this type of counseling in Chapter 7). In the first card, her attention was drawn to the nature scene surrounding the King of Coins. She said, "This is my *need to get back to nature, to a way of life that is meaningful.*" Thus began a discussion around what she wanted in a therapeutic practice as she *compared* it to her current job as a therapist.

The second card showed a golden castle in the background with a golden road winding up to it. Four wands were at the forefront of the picture with flower garlands strung between the tops. Judy saw this image as symbolic of reaching an ultimate *visionary goal*. Since she had mentioned that her work relationships didn't have the connection she wanted, I told her that the card also represents *people working together in harmony* and who also have similar values. "That is what *I want*," she said.

The third card showed a person wrapped up in a cloak, the only parts of him you could see were his *downcast eyes* and the top of his head. There were five cups at his feet, two were *upright* and three were *turned over*. Judy thought the person looked *depressed* and this card's image represented her *mood*. I suggested that the three cups that were over turned could represent her *disappointments*. I said, "Alternately, the full upright cups represent your talents and gifts that are there for you to use, to get what you want."

On her note pad, I directed her make a list of her gifts and talents. Judy wrote down several things that were positive about her abilities and then responded, "This is right on."

The fourth card contained the image of five *people struggling with each other* using long rods. She saw this card as the struggle she was in over her current vocation. The lower level of the *caretaking* archetype was *strong* in Judy and she felt *overly responsible to those clients who "needed her"* and *wondered* who would take care of them if she *quit*. She mentioned several other minor factors that were *keeping her from doing* what she really wanted to do.

Then, I pointed to the sliver of a *moon* in the sky of the Five of Cups and said, "The moon symbolically represents your *spiritual life* or the *feminine* side. The symptoms you are having are on your left side, which is the feminine side. The other set of symptoms you are having are at the *throat chakra* and the *root chakra*. I asked her, "What are they telling you?" Expertly, Judy said, "My symptoms are telling me to have the courage (spine) to search for the spiritual (left side of body) using my will (throat chakra) and take the first step (root chakra) towards what I want for myself."

The last card depicted the archetype of the Hierophant, a *traditional spiritual teacher*. The image on the card depicted a person with a jeweled headdress over a purple cap and cape with several traditional religious symbols. When Judy saw this image she talked about having the kind of practice where she could talk to her clients about their spirituality. She said, "This type of counseling is not *allowed* where I *work*."

Archetypes and Patterns of the Archetypes

In my assessment, the archetypes that Judy wanted for herself were present for her because she could verbalize what she *wanted*, but she was not *developed* enough to actualize them at the levels she wanted to express them in her practice. She did hear the message of the Tarot reading and said she would begin to do what was needed to accomplish her dream of becoming a holistic therapist.

> Her first step was to take classes to learn more about inner work. "I want to make sure I am the kind of person I want to be before I make the leap." She paused, looked down at her hands that were folded in her lap and said, "I am *not ready*."
>
> Judy's ideal was to be a *spiritual teacher* to her clients. Realistically, she knew she needed to travel further down her own *spiritual path*, towards her own healing before she could *teach* others about this complicated inner territory that is filled with archetypes of all kinds.
>
> Judy took the higher path of the archetypes operating in her and began classes that taught her to know and heal herself and thus *safely* started working toward her dream. The surgery was successful, correcting the physical complications; the symptoms in her neck resolved as well. During her *healing journey* she made the effort to *encounter* the archetypes of *transformation* that helped her *grow and develop* higher levels of *consciousness*.

Would she have healed as well without the counseling and clarification of her issues? During counseling she was guided towards her own conclusions and thus her own plan. She may very well have eventually reached these conclusions by herself. However, the counseling sped up her insights, which in turn probably had a direct effect on her immediate condition and her eventual recovery.

The archetypes listed below are a few of the many ancient patterns that exist in the human consciousness. Although it is impossible to list every archetype that exists, you can use the ones listed here to familiarize yourself with a few so that you learn to identify them. As you look over the list, consider your *sense* of the archetype. What does it feel like and where in your body do you feel it. Does the characteristic include a smell or a color? Does the archetype have a movement? What does it say to you personally? You may also disagree with my placement and labeling of the archetypes. Have fun forming you own philosophy. Make your own list and share them with others who are interested in this type of learning.

Largest Archetypes

These are easily identified because their attributes are found everywhere in the material and psychic world.

Masculine–Feminine

Large Archetypes

The large archetypes are prominent in our daily lives.

Mother	Father	Child	Teacher	Student
Warrior	Death	Love	War	Peace
Grace	Chaos	Healer	Healing	Adult
Negative	Positive	Wisdom	Seeker	Logic
Intuition	Purity	Strength	Passion	Delusion
Fear	Courage	Creativity	Completion	Trust
Synthesis	Success	Failure	Light	Dark
Higher	Lower	Growth	Oppression	Freedom
Victim	Visionary	Chief	Storyteller	Slave
Scribe	Martyr	Aries	Taurus	Gemini
Leo	Virgo	Libra	Imagination	Consciousness
Hermit	Color	Trickster	Bully	God

Smaller Archetypes

These archetypes are smaller and not as easy to identify in our daily living. Basically, mirror neurons in our brain, enable us to empathize with each other and also enable us to *recognize* traits and actions that are found in all humans and as well as animals.

Familiar	Looking	Reported	Aloneness	Anxiety
Gentleness	Meaningful	Blockages	Stimulate	Breathe
Walk	Think	Meditation	Explore	Abruptly
Culmination	Complaining	Arguing	Order	Effective
Finished	Begin	Came	Went	Intention
Comparing	Wondering	Responsible	Disappointment	Transformation
Waiting	Gossip	Working	Fulfillment	Stealing
Communications	Insights	Endings	Beginnings	Kneeling

Archetypes and Patterns of the Archetypes 99

Archetypal Scenarios

Short story-like phrases that give information about our thinking, behaving, feeling, and intentions towards each other have been with humanity since the beginning. While looking over these scenarios, imagine the ancient cave dweller. Did they use these archetypes?

Sharing with others	Distress over a lack of courage	Brief relaxation phase
Lack of will	Conversations	Use on your own
Speaking your truth	Need to get back to nature	People working together cooperatively
Body language	Moving on	Happy family
Healing journey	Pause to look and evaluate	Planning for the future
Holding onto something	Preparing a meal	Prayer and meditation
Leaving a situation	Victorious homecoming	Grief over loss
Generosity towards others	Waiting for help	Making choices
Carrying a burden	Working at your bliss	Committing to a relationship
Rejoicing with others	Making associations	Stealing from others

Patterns in the Life Story

Hinduism and Buddhism teach that the soul must pass through many lifetimes; each one teaching needed lessons, until the soul reaches perfection so that it can ascend to a higher level eventually re-uniting with the living *Source of Life*. There are numerous examples of this type of rebirth in the Hebrew Bible/Old Testament. History records show that the early Christian church believed in reincarnation and of the soul's journey back to oneness with God. This all changed by Imperial decree some 500 plus years after the death of Christ. Emperor Justinian in 545 A.D. was able to apply the full power of Rome and his authority to stop the belief in reincarnation.

Given the many theories and compelling stories that indicate we have lived past lives, I feel we must give this idea consideration when dealing with clients. Although I have done past-life regressions, and come up with several archetypal patterns that are replaying in my present life, I have very little physical evidence of a past life. I do know that regressions can be therapeutic in treating present life issues and therefore have therapeutic value. Here is my simple take on a very complicated and maybe unknowable phenomenon—what happens after we die.

If you look at the events of your lifetime, it will have segment upon segment of little clips of scenarios that can be found universally. In theory, the reincarnation of our soul and the possibility of individual karma will produce an earthly drama that will take on long patterns that have been played out by us since the beginning. When you get really good at making associations between your present-life patterns, you can imagine what other lifetimes must have looked like just by examining the patterns in this life. For instance, in one lifetime, I was my own paternal grandfather. Since, in that lifetime, I died when my son was very young, the theme was that I had been born to him, in this life, so that I might *"finish my parental responsibility and take care of him."* Shortly after the regression, I relayed this information to my father and step-mother. My step-mother exclaimed, "Well, you certainly have taken care of him!" My father then brought out an old picture of his father (which would have been me in another life). On the back of the picture, my grandfather had written the name of the town where he lived at that time of the photograph. Because he was fairly unschooled, he had misspelled the town's name of Tenino and spelled it *Toni*no. We were surprised to find my name on the back of the picture. There was a silence in the room as we all pondered this *mistake*.

Basically, my karmic pattern with my father was one of *finishing my responsibility* and *caring for my child*. In this lifetime, it felt like a long exercise in *forgiveness as one forgives a child* or *unconditional love*. I am grateful that my open-mindedness, about other perspectives, that included reincarnation, helped me have a good relationship with my immature father. Maybe we polished up our souls and our karma too.

Reincarnation is practically virgin territory as a topic of mainstream conversation. Who among us is going to say we don't continue our life story after we die? If that is conceivable, then who among us is going to deny that we may be able to live another life in the body? Reincarnation is like a continuing life story with twists and turns and drama. In other words, we may live out archetypal scenarios even after we die. Of course, we need to keep in mind that just because something seems logical, doesn't mean it is an actuality.

Archetypal scenarios are especially obvious during relationship games. It seems that a large portion of our life is involved in playing games with one another. Parental game is one thing, but romantic games seem to hold a lot of emotional energy for moving one's psyche along the path to maturity. They can be played as dysfunctional games that include the archetype of chaos, where everything seems to go wrong. On the other hand, the games may be of a harmonic higher order with cooperation and respect as the main pattern of the relationship. Consider these scenarios:

At the lower levels we see *she/he done me wrong, he's not the man I married, unrequited love, jealousy games, rejection, disappointment*, and *the lover's quarrel*.

At the higher levels we play out scenarios like: *we're so in love, life committed to family and others* which may include a positive side of *martyrdom*.

Using hypnotic techniques, you can regress a person and identify troubling patterns in a past life. The scenarios found in the previous lifetime usually contain karmic reasons for your actions in this lifetime. These reasons come to you during the meditative process and for years after the experience. Regression is one of those experiences that are multiple-leveled and it is best to study the teaching of the story until you feel done. Sessions of this kind can lead directly to a therapeutic resolution or, simply, an easier-to-live-with perspective.

My paternal grandmother first introduced me to the idea of reincarnation as a child. In my late twenties, and because my young son was killed in a car accident, I had an intense need to learn about life after death. I formally began this part of my education by reading everything I could find about the life and work of the Christian mystic Edgar Cayce. His theories dovetailed with the philosophies of contemporary mystic and transpersonal psychologist, Richard Alpert or Ram Dass. I read many other accounts of life after death, reincarnation, and spirituality during my twenties and so began my archetypal journey to better understand myself and my world.

During those years, I used the songs of Bob Dylan as a therapeutic comfort. Poet and author Kahlil Gibran spoke to me richly of everyday life experiences, which he wrote in a way that exposed life as holy. I also used self-help and metaphysical books by authors such as Wayne Dyer, Mathew Fox, Dan Millman and Deepak Chopra. I even managed to procure samples of the consciousness expanding drugs of the era. Like many of my generation, I was intrigued with the philosophies of the 70s and 80s, and as an *archetypal seeker*, I had a strong need to know what we were and why we were here.

All of the possibilities in all the books I have read, my own mystical or peak experiences, and what others have imparted to me over the years, are a part of my thinking. At this time, I look at my world and see patterns everywhere in the lives of the ordinary person and those people in the news and in history. I am convinced that once we are adept at seeing these patterns, we can use these patterns to give us information about what we need to know to live our lives more fully.

Observing and using archetypal patterns is a long and complicated journey of awareness that takes much focus and study. One must have the *desire* to see the world of patterns and understand their purpose while at the same time, be able to use that information in your daily life. It is a journey that is well worth the time and effort, for the patterns are an incredible show of creativity and structure that we are all lovingly a part of here and now.

Chapter 7
Archetypal Tools for Healing in the 21st Century

*The Living Temple Has
Imagination, Sensation, Awareness
—and It Heals*

Counselor Know Thyself

The ability to recognize yourself in the archetypes is at the foundation for competence with tools that make use of the archetypes. Only when you begin to identify archetypal patterns and their expressions in your own life can you hope to use the tools that work with archetypes in a therapeutic session.

One way to use the larger archetypes is to think of them as inner and outer guides on your journey of self-discovery. These energetic forces each exemplify a way of being in the world and their attributes are available to be expressed through our personalities. Accordingly, we experience the archetypes as a result of our own predominant perspective. For instance, spiritual seekers embody saints, gods, and goddesses, while academics and other rationalists conceive of the archetypes as the invisible patterns in the mind that control how we experience the world. Scientists see the archetypes as holographic impressions of the universe. Scholars of psychology study archetypes by examining their presence in art and literature and by comparing them to similar imagery that has existed throughout time. World wide, we find the archetypal symbols in our imagination, dreams, fantasies, and in the world of the arts, myth, legend, literature, and religion. Each archetype is expressed on many different levels and the expression and interpretation is dependent upon the physical, cognitive, emotional and spiritual development of the individual ego.

In my alternative nursing practice, I use the following therapeutic tools that are briefly discussed as an overview. All make use of the everlasting archetypes.

Dream Work

Dream images are thought to come from a level of consciousness Freud called the unconscious mind. Before Freud, mystics of antiquity described the attributes of this same consciousness and called it soul. Any way you want to look at it, nighttime dreaming is done at a level of consciousness that contains a universe of symbols and abstract realities. The unconscious mind is described exquisitely in psychologist Robert Johnson's book *Inner Work*. He explains that our unconscious mind is full of energies, forces, forms of intelligence, and distinct personalities that live within and through us. It is a large realm and one that has a complete life of its own running parallel to the ordinary life we live, this place in us is the source of much of our thoughts, feelings, and behaviors. It influences us in ways that are all the more powerful because it is unconscious. An example of the unconscious working in your life might be when a sudden insight about an issue that you have been struggling with, whether it be with an image or a plan, suddenly arises from your imagination and inspires you into action.

In working with nighttime dreams, I find that the unconscious mind has a dynamic relationship with the most conscious part of us—the ego. It reflects and validates our waking reality when we are whole and centered and compensates and corrects when the personality becomes too one-sided. Learning the art of dream work helps the dreamer to think and work symbolically with the emotional and physical events in life. Dreams hold information about spiritual realities, self-development, mythological archetypal themes, and the health of the mind and body. Dream research and contemporary techniques for remembering and analyzing dreams help clients achieve health and wholeness through a deeper understanding of themselves.

Freud thought dreams held sexual meaning, Adler believed they represented a struggle for identity, and Jung saw universal archetypes or basic patterns of human behavior. Others have seen existential meanings for a dreamer's nighttime images. Often, advanced students of dream work explore things like a psychic or precognitive meaning for the future, information about the health of the physical body, and religious meaning in terms of spiritual realities.

Dreams can be symbolic sign posts that come in service to help evaluate healing. The dreamer is able to contact unrecognized emotions and subtle sensations about what is happening to the body during a period of injury or disease. Dreams can help people understand their reactions to treatment, express emotions, and rid themselves of negative impacts, thus relieving tensions. Dreams can teach you to contact the curative powers within your mind, obtain personal healing symbols, find creative solutions to difficulties, and assess progress in stages of healing. For example, people often report images of green plant growth in their dreams as they recover from illness or injury. Positive new growth in various forms is usually indicative of an inner and outer healing. Dreams of death are also an indication of transformation taking place in the healee. The healee should be encouraged to work with the dream images by drawing them (using art materials) or through other methods of contemplation. This can bring positive feelings to full flower and speed healing. If the dream symbol is particularly significant, one might encourage the client to work with the image or symbol for weeks or months for maximum benefit.

Symbolic Levels of Venus

The Roman Goddess, Venus, is symbolic of the feminine energies inherent in the world. The Greeks knew this energy as Aphrodite. This energy is expressed through every one of us. The following are examples of the levels of this archetype.

Venus Urania
Esoteric knowledge, divine love, the divine human

Intuitive Venus
Nurturing higher ideals, intuitive counseling, participation in the arts

Spiritual Venus
Divine love, purity, appreciation of beauty

Platonic Venus
Chastity, beauty, humanitarianism, harmony

Harmonic Venus
Care of humankind, cooperation, unity

Hedonistic Venus
Desire and fulfillment of the human animal

~*US News*, 2010 special edition

The meditative discipline required in the remembering and recording of dreams can lead to increasingly clear awareness of our subtle experiences both asleep and awake. If you take the time to contemplate and understand your dreams, you will find guidance, illumination, and attitudes for healing your ego's concerns by learning to express a deeper part of yourself. It is important to keep in mind that the full healing potential of dreams will not be realized unless they are followed by conscious efforts toward growth and development.

Archetypal Tools for Healing in the 21ˢᵀ Century

Six Basic Guidelines for Dream Work

Keep a dream journal beside your bed and write your dreams down immediately upon awakening. Write them in first person as if you are still in the dream. Give the dream a date and title. Notice the feeling, in the dream, and correlate it to what is happening in your waking life. Write your analysis after the dream entry. You may want to wait until later in the day, and after some contemplation, to give the dream an analysis.

All dreams come in the service of health and healing. If you experience a "bad dream," it is because dreams sometimes take on a dramatically negative form to get our attention when they have something important to impart.

Only the dreamer can know with any certainty what the meaning of the dream is. The certainty usually comes with an intuitive "ah-ha!" response and is the only reliable indicator that the message of the dream has been received by conscious awareness.

When working with others about their dreams, it is wise to preface your remarks with words to the effect that "if it were my dream, this what it would mean" and keep your commentary in the first person as much as possible. This is a polite and less invasive way to communicate to each other about the very personal information in the dream.

In a dream work group, all participants should agree to maintain confidentiality of all discussions involving dream work. Members should be free to discuss their experiences openly outside the group, provided no one else's dreams are identifiable in their stories.

Dreams can have more than one meaning, and dream images can have multiple layers of symbolic meanings.

~ Jeremy Taylor

Guided Imagery

Guided imagery is a natural therapy that accesses our preconscious level of consciousness. Imagery is a way that your mind stores, codes, and expresses information. Imagery consists of thoughts that you can smell, hear, see, and taste. It is an inner representation of your experience (or your fantasy). Inner imagery is full of archetypal content that manifests as your nighttime dreams, day dreams, memories, plans, possibilities, and projections. Imagery has been called the language of the arts, emotions, and the deeper self.

The therapist uses a progressive relaxation and hypnotic induction to place the client's mind in a state of relaxation in order to access the information buried in deeper levels of consciousness. Depending upon the intended outcome, imagery can then be facilitated by directive, or interactive techniques. Imagery is based on the process of imaginative information flowing to and from the various levels of consciousness of the healee. The healee gets involved with the imagery as a child would a bedtime story. The imagination comes up with a scenario, the mind is piqued and inner images are then utilized to help with relaxation and physiologic healing.

The images of our imagination are potent because they have been created from the depths of our emotions, and because they are formed by feelings, they evoke feelings. The symbols in the imagery contain the essence of the figure represented (i.e., the archetypal wise person, mother, father, animal or plant, etc.). The archetypal images can calm and reassure us; they can give us emotional strength as well as affect our body processes. Positive emotions, thoughts, and images have specific biochemical correlates that influence how the body works. Imagining the immune system functioning to perfection can counteract a life-threatening disease. By focusing attention on, and consciously directing imagination and emotions to different areas of the body, it is possible to actually alter the quality of blood flow, dilating or constricting blood vessels.

Guided imagery as a therapeutic intervention works because the images are novel stimuli and the body/mind becomes more alert and responsive to events that have new informational value. The images are known to facilitate mind modulation of the autonomic, endocrine, immune, and neuropeptide systems.

Guided imagery has over forty years of empirical research to support the fact that it facilitates the mind-body connection in healing. Virtually, no physical ailment is beyond this mind-body approach.

Archetypal Tools for Healing in the 21ST Century

Self-Guided Imagery Exercise

Sit or lay in a comfortable position with eyes closed. You may want to listen to soft music and allow the body to relax. During this time, you should focus your attention on your breathing. Then, when you feel ready, recall a pleasant memory. Look around the memory situation with your inner vision noticing the how you feel and any colors, textures, sounds, and smells that might be present. Do this for as long as you are comfortable. When you want to bring your consciousness back into the current time and place, simply open your eyes, move your body and take a few deep breaths.

Write about your imagery experience in your journal.

Tarot Counseling

Tarot, as we know it today, emerged from a collection of seventy-eight cards developed in the fifteenth century. The images on each card carry a rich symbolic tapestry of human experience. Many of the images in modern Tarot decks are derived from archetypal characters and symbols that can be found in the popular art of the Renaissance. When researching books on Tarot, we can find a variety of interpretations for the symbols and all of them are useful at some level.

Like the Rorschach inkblot test, Tarot does not easily lend itself to research purposes. Both Modalities lack the psychometric qualities that could be used to measure psychological variables, such as intelligence, aptitude, behavior, and emotional reaction. However, according to Tarot scholar Stewart Kaplin, this tool, like other tests, serves to elicit responses that can then be evaluated in standard diagnostic terms or other criteria. One example, Arthur Rosengarten, a transpersonal psychologist, conducted a pilot study with recovering perpetrators and/or victims of spousal abuse and family violence. Rosengarten analyzed the respective position of each card and assumed that every card in a spread stood for something in the individual's psyche, although multiple levels of meaning could be found in each card. In his book, *Tarot and Psychology*, Rosengarten concluded that the insights stimulated and clarified by Tarot are of primary value for the individual, not the method itself, and that Tarot must be considered an instrument of potential psychotherapeutic value in which the counselor seams together the nuances that gather meaningfully during a client's session.

Before a Tarot counseling session, the client is assessed for ego strength, cognitive abilities and emotional state. They must have the ability for insight or openness for new thinking, and an ability to follow a train of thought. The cards should not be used with those who have negative ideas about Tarot because by their own thinking they may see images on the cards in a pessimistic way.

When working with archetypal imagery of any kind it is best to, primarily, rely upon the personal projections of the client because as they discuss what they see in the imagery, the therapist gets a glimpse of deeply personal information from which to begin forming assessments and begin to plan for future interventions and potential outcomes. When the client is finished *free associating* or telling what they see in the cards, if appropriate, the counselor then can give his or her interpretation of the image all the while watching the client's responses closely. By watching and listening for subtle nuances such as facial expression, body language and voice intonation the counselor learns a great deal about a person in a single session.

Counselors who become skilled in the art of Tarot counseling use the cards in self-development, client assessment, and as a complementary therapy with wellness counseling clients. Likewise, it is utilized with some mental health clients as the licensed psychotherapist gain insights into his/her client and help them better understand their issues. Generally, counselors would not use Tarot imagery with acute care patients because they may be in a survival state of mind and may not be receptive to insights.

Archetypes in Your Life

The art on Tarot decks is an easy way to identify and experience the archetypes in your living. Using a Tarot deck of your choice, draw one card a day and meditate upon the images in the card. Read the author's symbolic interpretation of the artwork. How does this archetype manifest in your life? Keep going until you have gone through the entire deck.

Humanistic Astrology

Astrology can be viewed as a language of archetypal principles, a way of perceiving form and order in the life of an individual, and a way of symbolizing each person's oneness with these principles. The astrologer understands that the individual is a unique form expressing a unique relationship with the world. Every individual is considered a whole and unique expression of universal principles, patterns, and energies.

The Zodiac was considered by ancient astrologers and philosophers as the "soul of nature," that which gave form and order to life. An astrological chart portrays the positions and interrelations of the moving planets such as the sun and the moon, measured against the backdrop of the fixed stars in the heavens. At its foundation, astrology correlates what is happening in the heavens to the agricultural year with its seasonal tasks and considerations. The system is based on natural experience and not simply an intellectual abstraction. Keeping track of the heavens is one of the oldest sciences humanity possesses.

In modern terms, astrologers consider the universe as one whole process that consists of innumerable interpenetrating fields of energy. For instance, the energy field of any individual is related intimately to the larger energy field of his or her cosmic environment.

Through an understanding of the universal factors operating in us, we can attain a greater understanding of the universal principles of life itself. Science accepts cardiographs, and encephalographs as useful tools, both of which are relatively unique manifestations of human energies and rhythms. The astrological birth chart is the graph through which the cosmos enables us to understand its archetypal energies and rhythms, and particularly how they operate within each of us.

Astrology has been defined as astronomy applied for psychological purposes. The horoscope interpreted by a skilled astrologer not only provides a picture of the person's hereditary inclinations, but points to latent potentials, and suggests directions of needed growth. It gives a symbolic map of the process of self-actualization.

Currently, many professionals explore astrology's usefulness in health care practices. Some have found astrology useful in experiential techniques of psychotherapy such as primal therapy, rebirthing, holotropic breathwork and psychospiritual crises.

Additionally, there are many computer programs that contain the complicated data required to draw up an individual chart. I use one such system and can print off an individualized astrological chart that shows the position of the planets at the time of a client's birth. This circular graph, called a natal chart, helps me correlate possible archetypal influences and potentials. During sessions with clients, I may do a systematic analysis of each of the planets and their placement of the natal chart. As with any intuitive process, the value of my interpretation is verified by the client. During this interactive process, I can assess a great deal about who they are and what archetypal forces are prominent in their personality.

The most meaningful part of the session is that, as we study this symbolic art, and we search the heavens for understanding, we begin to feel a unity with the whole cosmos. The how and why of astrology may not be as important as the knowing that we have a *divine connection* to the whole. For as we look to the heavens for answers to life's challenges, we begin to see ourselves in the stars and eventually come to *know deeply* that we are indeed a part of all creation.

Art on Cards

Most of us don't have cathedrals with artistic murals on the walls for the benefit of our clients. However, we can find decks of cards with symbols and expressive images. Three such decks are *Soul Cards* by Deborah Koff-Chapin, *Animal Spirits Knowledge Cards* by Susan Seddon Boulet, and *Tao Oracle: An illuminated new approach to the I-Ching* by Ma Deva Padma.

The *Soul Cards,* which come in two decks of sixty cards each, also carry depictions of archetypal forces and may be used in the same way as Tarot cards. I have found them useful with people who are uncomfortable with Tarot. However, unlike Tarot, they don't have an underlying structure. For that reason, I find them more difficult to work with than Tarot cards. Nonetheless, the cosmic law of synchronicity, or meaningful coincidence, also works with these cards.

From Ms. Koff-Chapin's web site:

> When a card is chosen in association with a question, the image often evokes immediate insight. The guidebook supports you to use your creative resources to delve into the images through journal writing, storytelling, visualization, movement, dream incubation and other expressive modalities. When used

Archetypal Tools for Healing in the 21ST Century

in relationships and groups, Soul Cards catalyze refreshing responses and authentic communication. Children are fascinated with the images, and often verbalize with unexpected wisdom and maturity. Soul Cards are used by: therapists, coaches, workshop leaders, spiritual directors, healers, and intuitives as well as in management meetings, hospitals, spiritual retreats, and creative writing groups.

The *Animal Spirits Knowledge Cards* are a collection of forty-eight paintings of animal spirit beings. I use these in a session when a client may need a symbol to take with them for use in various ways. After the card is picked by the client, I scan it and print it to a larger size and send a copy away with them.

The images on the cards are magical, mystifying creatures often part animal and part human. The images are fantastic creatures that are exceedingly powerful, they are beings that are the spirit guides who lead the departed to the next life, they restore balance and harmony to a troubled world, and they heal the sick. Tribal shaman knew the animal spirits well, and they would journey beyond ordinary reality to invoke their power. These cards have the image on one side and the title, symbology, keywords and a short description of the animal in myth and nature on the other side. To the ancients, all things in nature had spiritual and sacred meaning.

The *Tao Oracle* is a deck of sixty-four cards with artwork and a book of writings that reflect a Taoist philosophy. The author's images are beautiful and the book contains a perspective that stimulates your mystical archetype. This work is Ma Deva Padma's interpretation of the centuries-old Chinese book of *I-Ching*. She believes that, because it is a work from the heart, it is therefore in accordance with the Tao. After working with this tool for several years, I think she is right; she has created a master tool.

I use this artistically decorated deck of cards differently than I use Tarot, although one could certainly use them in a layout. (There are several layouts for their use in the book that comes with the deck.) I have the client meditate upon their question, while holding the cards and slowly shuffling. Once they have their question firmly in mind, they will draw a card and then they are asked to quietly read the interpretation from the book. It never fails to "hit the nail on the head." Of course if you wanted to find the right card using the coins and yarrow stick method, you can do that, too. Make a ceremony out of it.

By adding information, while under the gentle influence of meditation, to the original messages offered in the I Ching, the author of the Tao Oracle created an enriching vehicle for those striving for self-awareness. It can facilitate your acceptance of change—however the winds of change may be blowing in your life. The wisdom of the Tao, as portrayed in this deck and book, is highly relevant today because all of the scenarios she writes about are archetypal. The wisdom the inquirer receives is a broader perspective on the dynamics influencing his or her life at the moment. This little deck freely offers its insights to the sincere seeker.

The following are activities that stimulate archetypal expression.

Artistic Expression and Creative Projects

The imagination bridges the unconscious and the conscious realms. Images, metaphors, and symbols carry and translate messages between the outer world and the personal, cultural, and universal layers of our inner world. We are all artists and can work with artistic materials. Something remarkable happens when we tap into inner creative resources; the psychological journey to wholeness begins and one experiences the movement of consciousness as it flows through the hands and is verified by the eyes.

The simple project of doodling in a diary once a day can have profound effects. I use art expression as homework assignments for clients. It can release difficult life experiences and offer them up to be healed during the session. There are multiple projects that can be searched out and utilized to bring insights to consciousness.

Much can be accomplished with writing, journaling, and poetry. Words, as well as images, are full of the archetypes waiting for the artist to give them expression. When we allow the material deep within to emerge, it can be a wonderful teaching. It is important to allow ourselves to consciously commune with the symbol or image as it emerges from the unconscious mind because this act of child-like play deepens our experience and we begin the healing process. This kind of work resembles meditation and helps you get in touch with many archetypal aspects of yourself. When you embark upon this work, your entire person and the creative tools becomes a vehicle for the symbol to move from the unconscious to consciousness, from the unknown to the known.

Archetypal Tools for Healing in the 21st Century

Eventually, as we work with our hands, we begin to observe recurring images, ideas, colors, shapes, and textures and we begin to recognize them as our self making itself known through our unique mythology and drawings. The imagination is given to us to nourish our soul on its journey. Keep your art alive by acknowledging the images by writing and talking about them, and if it is an abstract idea, by your drawings. Begin using your personal symbols in your conversations with others. If we are open to them, the inner images are our keepers and our guides on this long, often arduous journey we call life.

Geometry of the Self

What geometric shapes would you associate with your life's journey: a square, triangle, circle, spiral, semicircle, octagon, or cross? Meditate on your chosen shape. What colors come to mind? As you meditate upon your personal history, what do you associate with this color. Write your thoughts down. Now, meditate on the colors and observe the feelings and situations that are attached to the color. Draw/paint these symbols using the colors you thought of. When finished put your painting before you and meditate upon it. Explore others' interpretations of your chosen shape and color. Begin building your interpretation and write about it in your journal.

Movement and Dance

Much can be said about movement, dance, and the mind-body connection as a form of archetypal rhythm and direction. Energy flows through our bodies but gets blocked for various negative reasons. A helpful meditation is to imagine the flow of energy through your body to and from the larger universe.

Our body's movement involves a complex interaction of mental, physical, and spiritual processes. As we move, our unconscious feelings and memories will bubble up to be acknowledged and worked with. For example, the mind stores mental images, while the body stores memories at the level of feeling. If you did a dance that included motions by the arms and chest (heart chakra), the movement may release memories of how you were taught to love.

It seems when certain parts of the body are opened by movement, stories and experiences emerge. Consequently, when we listen to our bodies and move accordingly, we clear out our body-house of negativity. When we are clear on our life's issues, we are healthier, more aware and efficient—everything we do improves.

Movement Meditation

Choose a music that helps you become quiet and reflective. Begin to move around the room, allowing your body to move aimlessly to the music. You might want to expand with the out-breath and contract with the in-breath. As you move, notice what comes up for you mentally and emotionally. After you have moved freely for a few minutes, close your eyes and slowly explore different body postures that express different experiences. You may wish to combine these postures so that your movement becomes your own ritual dance, one that tells a story about your life.

Afterward, write down your thoughts and drawings in a journal.

Archetypal Energy Work

Hands on manipulation for energy healing date back 3,000 years to China, but may be much older than that. Touch and the "laying on of hands" are human intuitive tendencies that are archetypal and found in every culture.

There are a number of techniques. Some are known by names such as acupuncture, Therapeutic Touch, Healing Touch, and Reiki. It is helpful for the professional to be trained in one of these modalities. After you have practiced for a while, you tend to go your own way and form your own style. The overall effect is that energy treatments relieves pain and boosts the immune system to speed healing. For example, I use my hands as sensors to assess and balance the energy field surrounding the body. I sense energy blockages around the body and, at the same time, healing energy flows through me to the client. The majority of client's report feeling deeply relaxed and some fall asleep—or are energized. During this energy meditation, I *trust* that they will get the exact amount of energy they need.

Energy Prayer

Gain the client's permission to do energy work. Give them a brief explanation about energy and their body. The experience of energy worker will vary each according to his or her own understanding. For instance, during the prayer, I envision a white or gold energy coming through my crown chakra and that flows out my hands. The energy feels like gentle warm water running through a hose.

Prepare by composing a short silent prayer. Open your prayer with words that reflect your deepest spiritual self. (This will be different for everyone.) Ask for protection against all negative energy. Next, ask for healing energy to pour through your body for the benefit of your client, mentioning his/her name. Then begin to work in whatever way seems best. At this point you are working free form. You may want to ask the healee where he or she needs to be touched. When you feel done, leave the healee to continue the meditation for as long as they want. Tell them that they can slowly bring their consciousness back to the room when they are ready.

End with running water over your hands as an energy cleansing. Imagine your body's energies groomed and in harmony.

Working with the flow of energy through the body promotes healing. This energy can be directed or encouraged to move through and around the body in such a way as to have an impact on the physical structure and functioning of the body. Healing energy can be accessed to work with our emotional well-being as well. Energy work may involve hands-on contact or may be done with no contact with the physical body. A typical session may last any where from ten to thirty minutes during which one can stand, sit in a chair, or lie down.

It is as important for people to develop awareness that the quality of energy flow in and around their body is just as important to physical health and psychological well-being as the flow of breath. In my practice, because I cannot be with them at all times, I teach clients to do their own energy work. Although there are multiple techniques (mentioned above) that teach energy healing, it doesn't need to be complicated.

Bottom line: During the session, the energy worker's activities promote a meditative trance. At this time, the healee's meditative state deepens and complements the body's own natural ability to heal. The client and the energy worker become like energy receptive sponges as the energy is manipulated for the benefit of the client. The energy worker also receives the healthy benefits of working with a spiritual energy.

New Rules in Health Care

We are in the process of creating a new vision of health care. However, in order to do so, it is necessary to connect all parts of the health care system and to creatively integrate the similar and the dissimilar. Everyone benefits from traditional medical interventions. Nevertheless, there is a place in the whole for alternative and complementary therapies. In some areas of the country, empirically proven modalities are being embraced in integrated clinics. We still have a way to go. In the next leg of our journey, the health industry needs to recognize and fully integrate humanities' older healing arts such as astrology, dream work, and Tarot interpretation and so on. So, let the discussions begin.

The new rules call for unconditional acceptance and caring for the whole person. Some believe that this includes the acceptance of archetypal patterns inherent in the human race. From one perspective, we must live through the presenting disease or injury and *learn from it* rather than just going in for the "fix." This perspective postulates that everyone needs to explore the complexities of life however painful. It is only by facing our shadows, or our darker side, that we begin to heal.

Nurse theorist Martha Rogers was one of the contemporary thinkers who brought forth the olden idea that disease is a meaningful reflection of the whole person. She thought that health and illness should be viewed equally as each is an expression of the life process and that the meaning to be derived from disease states comes from an understanding of the life process in its totality. In other words, pain and disease carry symbolic information that can help people integrate their life experiences. We know that that holistic counseling facilitates psychological and spiritual growth. We also know that this treatment optimizes the outcome and the client has a better chance to heal.

Archetypal Tools for Healing in the 21ST Century

With the above mentioned tools, it is possible to move ourselves and others to a higher developmental level of consciousness. At this new level, the disease may be relinquished and the person healed. However, if this is not possible and the disease persists, the expansion of consciousness still occurs and is on-going no matter the circumstances. The expansion of consciousness is healthy and it just is. No conditions should be placed on this natural process. It is ongoing in each of us. If you consider the difference between the levels of consciousness inherent in the archetypes, the individual's karma and the multitude of ways that our life paths take, you have to know that we cannot comprehend the entirety of the All That Is. One thing seems certain: because we exist, the urge toward wholeness is a part of us and all of Nature. To us, this archetypal force is known as growth or expansion. The ancient Greek philosophers knew this urge as physis.

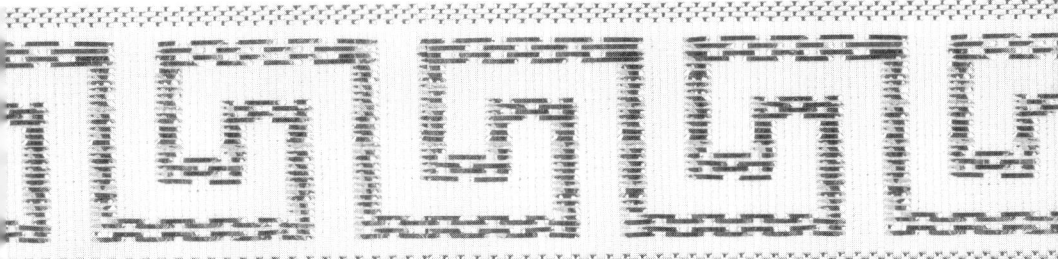

Epilogue
References and Recommended Reading

The archetypes are thought to be cosmic forces that are without form until they get expressed through the natural world—of which we are a part. In this book, I have given you the basic intellectual knowledge necessary to begin your exploration of the archetypes. You have been introduced to several tools and exercises that give you methods with which to continue your developmental journey. It is difficult to fully understand the intellectual concepts until you work with them. For only when you have learned how to see the archetypes in your own experience, will you more fully know them when you see them in others.

Work with these tools with an open and receptive mind, paying close attention when you work with your hands. Your hands are an extension of the heart chakra and a feeling part of yourself. Observe and acknowledge their creativity in action.

Go for walks. Look for patterns in nature that can be found throughout the world and the universe. The patterns in nature—cloud swirls for instance—are perfect examples of the energy of an archetype in motion (in this case, the cosmic energy behind the movement of the wind). Once you begin to regularly notice the patterns, there is no going back. You will see your oneness with everyone and everything in our world, a family of forces or energies that make up our universe. What greater gift than to see the hand of creation and to *know*, to the depths of your being, that you are part of the All That Is.

What About Billie?

Billie, the friend I mention in the Introduction, who wondered about the traditional path I was about to embark upon some forty years ago, now lives in a historic Victorian home in a small town near me. Though she is a busy video producer, copyeditor and photographer, Billie still surrounds herself with a garden and dozens of antique rose bushes—still drinks herbal tea, and is still up for an occasional conversation about where we've been and where we're each headed.

Recently, during a soft summer evening with an occasional autumn breeze, Billie and I relaxed beside my organic vegetable garden. We talked quietly and reminisced about our lives.

"I was right, wasn't I," Billie said smiling over her cup of tea. "No matter how you tried to fit yourself onto the traditional path of nursing, by your very inquiring nature, you always managed to veer off on paths less traveled. You took the best of what traditional nursing had to offer, but unfailingly added your own unique touches–until the end result has been decidedly alternative."

"True," I nodded thoughtfully, "my path has been strewn with difficulties—I suppose because I didn't seem to fit the mold of 'institutional nurse,' but I eventually did find my own unique expression in nursing, didn't I?"

"I've watched you," Billie said, "with deep interest and admiration as you blazed your own trail through what was pretty much uncharted wilderness at the time. You literally carved out a place for yourself to stand that more closely resonates with your understanding of the universe. And, I must say, the nursing profession is probably better for it…"

I chuckled as I saw myself from my long-time friend's point of view. "Yes," I said, "my nursing education turned out to be golden, I use it every day." I paused and then continued, "and, you know what, it's all been good." I sighed contentedly as I put my feet up on nearby stool, and leaned back into my comfortable chair. "Because of the trouble, I have learned to meet my challenges and not shrink from them. Overall, this generated a change in how I see the world."

The way I see it, in order to grow to one's potential, each of us must endure the demands of our life's path. As we go along, it seems that we are faced with choices that are like forks in the road. We can either take the high road that includes authenticity and integrity, or succumb to the low road with its negative thinking and behaving.

Even when circumstances seemed really dire, my aim has been to stay positive and choose the high road. Because of that attitude, my personal and professional life has turned out splendidly. I believe that walking the higher path gives one a Grace-filled life no matter what the challenges.

Billie and I discussed philosophy and religion for a while and then agreed that, whatever the reality of our living; it is and has been incredibly interesting—and fun.

To wrap up, I would like to leave you with a healing tool, a meditation, to use for personal relaxation and inspiration. You may also guide a friend through the introspective passages to help them experience their inner archetypes first hand.

Healing Place Meditation

Close your eyes and center your self in a resting posture. Bring your attention to the breath. Breathe in healing energy and relaxation and on the out breath let go of negativity. Meditate like this for a few minutes until your body feels relaxed and your mind receptive.

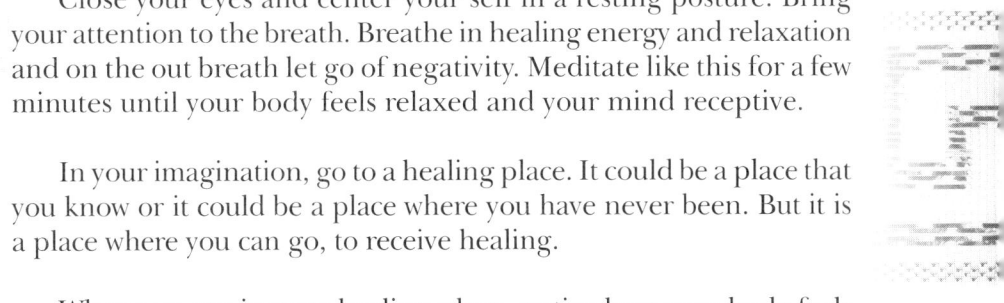

In your imagination, go to a healing place. It could be a place that you know or it could be a place where you have never been. But it is a place where you can go, to receive healing.

When you are in your healing place, notice how your body feels in the surroundings. Look around you, noticing the colors, sounds, textures, and any smells that may be in this place. Spend some time just being there. Take all the time you need. When you are ready, meditate upon your deepest spiritual value. It can be a word or a feeling. Trust that something will come to mind. (And if nothing comes to mind, that is okay, too.) Focus upon that word or feeling, letting everything else go. Spend some time with this thought or feeling.

When you are ready, bring that thought or feeling with you when you bring your consciousness back to the room.

Make a commitment to use this deep value with everyone you meet. Maybe, just maybe, you will bring a little more healing into the world.

Continue to contemplate your inner experience and write about it in your journal.

Selected Bibliography

Achterberg, J. Lawlis, F. (1984). *Imagery and Disease: A diagnostic tool for behavioral medicine*. Champaign, IL: Institute for Personality and Ablility Testing.

Arrien, A. (1997). *Tarot Handbook: Practical applications of ancient visual symbols*. New York, NY: Jeremy P. Tarcher/ Putnam.

Dossey, B. and Keegan, L. (2009) *Holistic Nursing: A Handbook for Practice*.(5th ed) Sudbury, MA: Jones and Bartlett Publishers.

Eden, D. & Feinstein, D. (1999). *Energy Medicine*. New York, NY: Jeremy P Tarcher/Putnam.

Edinger, F.E.(1980). *Ego and Archetype: A fascinating synthesis of C. G. Jung's fundamental psychological concepts*. New York, NY: Penguin Books.

Edinger, F. E. (1999). *The Psyche in Antiquity: Early Greek philosophy*. Toronto, Canada: Inner City Books.

Edinger, F. E. (1999). *The Psyche in Antiquity: Book Two Gnosticism and Early Christianity*. Toronto, Canada: Inner City Books.

Gilbert, T. (2004) *Messages from the Archetypes: Using Tarot for healing and spiritual growth*. Ashland, OR: White Cloud Press.

Gilbert, T. (2002, Sept). *The spiritual art of working with dreams. Journal of Holistic Nursing*. Thousand Oaks, CA: Sage Publishing.

Goswami, A. (1995). *The Self-Aware Universe: How consciousness creates the material world*. New York, NY: Jeremy P. Tarcher/Putnam.

Hillman, J. (1997). *Archetypal Psychology: A brief account.* Woodstock, CT: Spring Publications, Inc.

Johnson, R. (1986). *Inner work: Using dreams and active imagination for personal growth.* New York: HarperCollins.

Jung, C.G. (1990). *The Archetypes and the Collective Unconscious.* New York, NY: Princeton University Press.

Merritt, S. (1990) *Mind, Music and Imagery: Unlock your creative potential.* Plume/Penquin Books.

Nelson, J. E. (1994) *Healing the Split: Integrating spirit into our understanding of the mentally ill.* Revised ed. New York, NY: State University of New York Press.

Newberg, A. Waldman, M. R. (2006). *Why We Believe What We Believe: Uncovering our biological need for meaning, spirituality, and truth.* New York, NY: Free Press.

Newberg, A. Waldman, M. R. (2009). *How God Changes Your Brain.* New York, NY: Ballantine Books.

Newman, M. A. (1999). *Health as Expanding Consciousness* (2nd ed). New York, NY: National League for Nursing Press.

Pearson, C.S. (1991). *Awakening the Hero's Within: Twelve archetypes to help us find ourselves and transform our world.* San Francisco, CA: Harper.

Pierce, A. (1989) *Expressive Movement: Posture and action in daily life, sports and the performing arts.* Insight books.

Ray, P. H. & Anderson, S. R. (2000). *The Cultural Creatives: How 50 Million people are changing the world.* New York, NY: Three Rivers Press.

Rosengarten, A. (2000). *Tarot and Psychology: Spectrums of Possibility.* St. Paul, MI: Paragon House.

Samuels, M., Rockwood Lane, M. (1998). *Creative Healing: How to heal yourself by tapping your hidden creativity.* San Francisco, CA: Harper San Francisco.

Scully, N. (2003) *Alchemical Healing: A guide to spiritual, physical, and transformational medicine.* Rochester, VT: Bear & Company.

Skinner, Stephen (2009). *Sacred Geometry: Deciphering the code.* New York, NY: Sterling Publishing.

Schwartz, G. Russek, L. (1999). *The Living Energy Universe: a fundamental discovery that transforms science & medicine.* Charlottesville, VA: Hampton Roads Publishing Co.

Thomson, S. A. (1990). *Cloud Nine: A dreamer's dictionary.* New York, NY: Harper Collins.

US News & World Report (2010). "Secrets of the Lost Symbol." Special edition.

Wauters, A. (2007). *Homeopathic Color & Sound Remedies.* Berkely, CA: Crossing Press.

Waldman, M. R. ed. (2002). *Lover: Embracing the passionate heart. Archetypes of the collective unconscious.* New York, NY: Jeremy P. Tarcher/Putnam.

Wilber, K. (2000). *Integral Psychology: Consciousness, spirit, psychology, therapy.* Boston, MA: Shambhala.

Astrology

Meyer, M.R. (2000). *A Handbook for the Humanistic Astrologer.* Lincoln, NE: toExcel.

Parker, J. & D. (2001). *Parker's Astrology: The definitive guide to using astrology in every aspect of your life.* New York, NY: DK Publishing.

Dreams

Garfield, P. (1991). *The healing power of dreams.* New York: Fireside.

Taylor, J. (1992). *Where people fly and water runs uphill.* New York: Time Warner.

Thomson, S. A. (2003). *Cloud Nine: A dreamer's dictionary.* New York, NY: Quill publishers.

Tarot

Gilbert, T. (2004) *Messages from the Archetypes: Using Tarot for healing and spiritual growth*. Ashland, OR: White Cloud Press.

Greer, M. K. (2004). "Tarot and Emotions Research Project Report." *Alternative Journal of Nursing*. [Online serial].

Kaplan, S. R. (1978). *The Encyclopedia of Tarot*. New York, NY: US Games Systems Inc.

Maxwell, J. (1992). *The Tarot: An indispensable aid for every serious student of the cards*. Essex, England: Saffron Walden.

Place, R. M. (2001). *A Gnostic Book of Saints*. St. Paul, MI: Llewellyn Publications.

Rosengarten, A. (2000). *Tarot and Psychology: Spectrums of possibility*. St. Paul, MN, Paragon House.

Thomson, S. A. (2003). *Pictures from the Heart: A Tarot dictionary*. New York, NY: St. Martin's Griffin.

Wang, R. (2001). *The Jungian Tarot and its Archetypal Imagery*. Columbia, MD, Marcus Aurelius Press.

Guided Imagery

Rossman, M. (2000). *Guided Imagery for Self Healing: An essential resource for anyone seeking wellness*. Second Edition. Novato, CA, New World Library.

Soul Cards: http://www.touchdrawing.com/index1.html